PRENTICE-HALL FOUNDATIONS OF PHILOSOPHY SERIES

Virgil Aldrich	PHILOSOPHY OF ART
William Alston	PHILOSOPHY OF LANGUAGE
Stephen Barker	PHILOSOPHY OF MATHEMATICS
Roderick Chisholm	THEORY OF KNOWLEDGE
William Dray	PHILOSOPHY OF HISTORY
Joel Feinberg	POLITICAL PHILOSOPHY
William Frankena	ETHICS
Martin Golding	PHILOSOPHY OF LAW
Carl Hempel	PHILOSOPHY OF NATURAL SCIENCE
John Hick	PHILOSOPHY OF RELIGION
John Lenz	PHILOSOPHY OF EDUCATION
Richard Rudner	PHILOSOPHY OF SOCIAL SCIENCE
Wesley Salmon	LOGIC
Jerome Shaffer	PHILOSOPHY OF MIND
Richard Taylor	METAPHYSICS

Elizabeth and Monroe Beardsley, editors

THEORY

OF KNOWLEDGE

FOUNDATIONS OF PHILOSOPHY SERIES

Roderick M. Chisholm

Brown University

PRENTICE-HALL, INC.   ENGLEWOOD CLIFFS, N.J.

THEORY OF KNOWLEDGE, Chisholm

FOUNDATIONS OF PHILOSOPHY SERIES

C-91400

Current printing (last digit):
19   18   17   16   15   14   13   12

PRENTICE-HALL   INTERNATIONAL,   INC.,   London

PRENTICE-HALL OF AUSTRALIA, PTY., LTD., Sydney

PRENTICE-HALL   OF   CANADA,   LTD.,   Toronto

PRENTICE-HALL OF INDIA (PRIVATE), LTD., New Delhi

PRENTICE-HALL   OF   JAPAN,   INC.,   Tokyo

To the memory of

Bernard K. Symonds

FOUNDATIONS

OF PHILOSOPHY

Many of the problems of philosophy are of such broad relevance to human concerns, and so complex in their ramifications, that they are, in one form or another, perennially present. Though in the course of time they yield in part to philosophical inquiry, they may need to be rethought by each age in the light of its broader scientific knowledge and deepened ethical and religious experience. Better solutions are found by more refined and rigorous methods. Thus, one who approaches the study of philosophy in the hope of understanding the best of what it affords will look for both fundamental issues and contemporary achievements.

Written by a group of distinguished philosophers, the Foundations of Philosophy Series aims to exhibit some of the main problems in the various fields of philosophy as they stand at the present stage of philosophical history.

While certain fields are likely to be represented in most introductory courses in philosophy, college classes differ widely in emphasis, in method of instruction, and in rate of progress. Every instructor needs freedom to change his course as his own philosophical interests, the size and makeup of his classes, and the needs of his students vary from year to year. The fifteen volumes in the Foundations of Philosophy Series—each complete in itself, but complementing the others—offer a new flexibility to the instructor, who can create his own textbook by combining several volumes as he wishes, and can choose different combinations at different times. Those volumes that are not used in an introductory course will be found valuable, along with other texts or collections of readings, for the more specialized upper-level courses.

ELIZABETH BEARDSLEY   MONROE BEARDSLEY

ACKNOWLEDGMENTS

I wish to express my indebtedness to the students with whom I have discussed these problems, to Herbert Heidelberger and Ernest Sosa for their criticisms of earlier versions of this book, to the editor of *Mind* for permission to reprint parts of my article "J. L. Austin's Philosophical Papers," and to the Polish Scientific Publishers in Warsaw for permission to reprint parts of my contribution to *The Foundation of Statements and Decisions*, edited by K. Adjukiewicz.

RODERICK M. CHISHOLM

CONTENTS

INTRODUCTION

Reflection upon the nature of our knowledge gives rise to a number of perplexing philosophical problems. These constitute the subject matter of theory of knowledge, or epistemology. Most of them were discussed by the ancient Greeks and there is little agreement even now as to how they should be solved or otherwise disposed of.

By describing the topics of the seven chapters that follow, we may convey in general just was these problems are.

(1) What is the distinction between knowledge and true opinion? If one man has made a lucky guess ("I would say that it is the seven of diamonds") but doesn't really know, and another man knows, but isn't saying, and doesn't need to guess, what is it that the second man has (if anything) that the first man does not? One may say, of course, that the second man has *evidence* and that the first man does not, or that something is *evident* to the one that is not evident to the other. But what is it to have evidence, and how are we to decide in any particular case whether or not we do have evidence?

These questions have their analogues in both moral philosophy and logic. What is it for an act to be *right* and how are we to decide in any particular case whether or not a given act is right? What is it for an inference to be *valid* and how are we to decide in any particular case whether or not a given inference is valid?

(2) Our evidence for some things, it would seem, consists of the fact that we have evidence for other things. "My evidence that he will keep his promise is the fact that he said he would keep his promise. And my evidence that he said he would keep his promise is the fact that. . . ." Must we say of everything for which we have evidence, that our evi-

1

dence for that thing consists in the fact that we have evidence for some other thing?

If we try Socratically to formulate our justification for any particular claim to know ("My justification for thinking that I know that *A* is the fact that *B*"), and if we are relentless in our inquiry ("and my justification for thinking that I know that *B* is the fact that *C*"), we will arrive, sooner or later, at a kind of stopping place ("but my justification for thinking that I know that *N* is simply the fact that *N*"). An example of *N* might be the fact that I seem to remember having been here before or the fact that something now looks blue to me.

This type of stopping place may be described in two rather different ways. We could say, "There are some things (e.g., the fact that I seem to remember having been here before) which are evident to me and which are such that my evidence for those things does not consist in the fact that there are certain *other* things that are evident to me." Or we could say alternatively, "There are some things (e.g., the fact that I seem to remember having been here before) which cannot *themselves* be said to be evident but which resemble what can be said to be evident in that they may function as evidence *for* certain other things." These two formulations would seem to differ only verbally. If we adopt the first, we may say that some things are *directly evident*.

(3) The things that we ordinarily say we *know* are not things that are thus "directly evident." But in justifying the claim to know any particular one of these things, we can be led back, in the manner described, to various things that *are* directly evident. Should we say, therefore, that the whole of what we know, at any given time, is a kind of "structure" having its "foundation" in what happens to be directly evident at that time? If we do say this, then we should be prepared to say just how it is that the foundation serves to support the rest of the structure. But this question is difficult to answer, for the support that the foundation gives would seem to be neither deductive nor inductive. That is to say, it is not the kind of support that the premises of a deductive argument give to their conclusion, nor is it the kind of support that the premises of an inductive argument give to their conclusion. For if we take as our premises the whole of what is directly evident at any time, we cannot formulate a good deductive argument, and we cannot formulate a good inductive argument, in which any of the things we ordinarily say we know appears as a conclusion. It may be, therefore, that in addition to the "rules of deduction" and the "rules of induction," there are also certain basic "rules of evidence." The deductive logician tries to formulate the first type of rule; the inductive logician tries to formulate the second; and the epistemologist tries to formulate the third.

(4) One may ask, "*What* do we know—what is the *extent* of our knowledge?" One may also ask, "How do we decide in any particular case *whether* we know—what are the *criteria*, if any, of knowing?" The "problem of the criterion" arises out of the fact that if we do not have the answer to the second pair of questions, then, it would seem, we have no reasonable procedure for finding out the answer to the first; and if we do not have the answer to the first pair of questions, then, it would seem, we have no reasonable procedure for finding out the answer to the second. The problem may be formulated more specifically for different subject matters—for example, our knowledge (if any) of "external things," "other minds," "right and wrong," the "truths of theology." Many philosophers, apparently without sufficient reason, approach some of these more specific versions of the problem of the criterion from one point of view, and others of them, from quite a different point of view.

(5) Our knowledge (if any) of what are sometimes called the "truths of reason"—the truths of logic and mathematics and what is expressed by, "A surface that is red all over is not also green"—provides us with a particularly instructive example of the problem of the criterion. Some philosophers believe that any satisfactory theory of knowledge must be adequate to the fact that some of the "truths of reason" are among the things that we know. But other philosophers formulate criteria of knowing which are such that, according to those criteria, the "truths of reason" as traditionally conceived are not among the things we know. Still others attempt to simplify the problem by saying that the so-called "truths of reason" actually pertain, somehow, only to the ways in which people think or to the ways in which they use their language. But once these suggestions are put precisely, they lose whatever plausibility they may seem at first to have.

(6) Other problems of the theory of knowledge might properly be called "metaphysical." These include certain questions about the ways in which things appear. The appearances that things present to us when, as we say, we perceive them, seem to be subjective in that they depend for their existence and nature upon the state of the brain. This simple fact has led philosophers, perhaps too readily, to draw somewhat extreme conclusions. Some have said that the appearances of external things must be internal duplicates of those things—that when a man perceives a dog, a tiny replica of the dog is produced inside his head. Others have said that external things must be quite unlike what we ordinarily take them to be—that roses cannot be red when no one is looking at them. Some have said that physical things must be made up, somehow, of appearances, and others have said that appearances must be made up, somehow, of physical things. The problem has even led

some philosophers to wonder whether there are any physical things, and it has led other philosophers, more recently, to wonder whether there are any appearances.

(7) The "problem of truth" may seem to be one of the simplest problems of the theory of knowledge. If we say of a man, "He believes that Socrates is mortal," and then go on to add, "And what is more, his belief is true," then what we have added, surely, is no more than that Socrates *is* mortal. And "Socrates is mortal" tells us just as much as does "It is true that Socrates is mortal." But what if we were to say of a man that some one of his beliefs is true, without specifying which belief? What property, if any, would we be ascribing to his belief?

Suppose we say, "What he is now saying is true," when what he is now saying happens to be that what *we* are now saying, whatever it is, is false. In this case, are we saying something that is true or are we saying something that is false?

Finally, what is the relation between conditions of truth and criteria of evidence? We have good evidence, presumably, for believing that there are nine planets. This evidence consists of various other facts we know about astronomy, but it does not itself include the fact that there are nine planets. It would seem to be logically possible, therefore, for a man to have good evidence for a belief which is, nevertheless, a belief that is false. Does this mean that the fact that there are nine planets, if it is a fact, is really something that cannot be evident? Should we say, therefore, that no one can really *know* that there are nine planets? Or should we say that, although it may be possible to know that there are nine planets, it is not possible to know that we know that there are nine planets? Or does the evidence that we have for believing that there are nine planets somehow guarantee that the belief is true and therefore guarantee that there are nine planets?

Such questions and problems as these constitute the subject matter of theory of knowledge. A number of them, as the reader will already feel, are simply the result of confusion; and once the confusions are exposed, the problems vanish. But others of them, as this book is intended to show, are somewhat more difficult to deal with.

KNOWLEDGE

AND TRUE OPINION

1

The problem
of the
Theatetus
In Plato's dialogue, the *Meno*, Socrates remarks: "That there is a difference between right opinion and knowledge is not at all a conjecture with me but something I would particularly assert that I know. There are not many things of which I would say that, but this one, at any rate, I will include among those that I know." [97C] The distinction would seem to be obvious. If one has knowledge, then one also has right or true opinion. But the converse is not true: one may have right or true opinion without having knowledge. Thus, we may guess correctly today, and therefore, have true opinion, but not know until tomorrow. Or we may have true opinion and never know at all.

In the *Theatetus*, Plato poses the following question: What is the distinction between knowledge and true, or right, opinion? He then sets out to "bring the many sorts of knowledge under one definition." [148E] It is doubtful that he succeeded and it is certain that we cannot do any better. But we may throw some light upon "the many sorts of knowledge," if we consider the difficulties that are involved in answering Plato's question.

One approach to the question, which Plato himself suggests, is to assume, first, that if one man knows and another man has true opinion but does not know, then the first man has everything that the second man has and something else as well. Then, having made this assumption, we ask: What is that which, when added to true opinion, yields knowledge? This approach to Plato's question may be put more schematically. The expression "S knows that h is true," where "S" may be replaced by a name or description of some person and where "h is true" may be replaced by a sentence such as "It is raining" or "Anaxagoras was a Greek philosopher," is assumed to tell us three different things:

5

1.   S believes that *h*

e.g., the person in question believes that it is raining, or believes that Anaxagoras was a Greek philosopher. It also tells us that

2.   *h* is true

e.g., that it is raining, or that Anaxagoras was a Greek philosopher. And finally, it tells us something else:

3.   ———.

Thus, we have a blank to fill. What shall we say of 3?

We may begin by approaching our problem in this way, keeping in mind the possibility that we should have begun in some other way.

We will find that most of the expressions that come to mind as possible candidates for 3 will be expressions that seem to leave us with our problem. For when we try to say what *they* mean, we again come back to "know."

Adequate evidence   It is often said that *adequate evidence* is that which, when added to true opinion, yields knowledge. May we fill in our blank, then, by saying "S has adequate evidence for *h*"?

Some have objected to this type of definition by saying: "Consider a man who has adequate evidence (not only has he heard the opinions of all the experts, but he has also had access to all of the evidence that they have had) and who believes what he does not because of the evidence that he has, but for some entirely frivolous reason (he follows what the tea leaves say). However good his evidence may be, such a man surely cannot be said to know, even if what he believes is true, for he hasn't recognized his evidence for what it's worth." But what this objection shows us, one could argue, is not that it is possible for a man with a true belief to have adequate evidence and at the same time not to know; it shows us, rather, that it is possible for such a man to have adequate evidence, and therefore, to know, but without *knowing* that he knows.

There are other reasons, however, for rejecting the definition.

For one thing, it is possible to add adequate evidence to true belief or opinion without obtaining knowledge. Many of those who predicted the election results correctly had adequate evidence—even at an early point in the campaign—for what they believed and predicted, but no one, at that time, knew that the predictions were true.

And for another thing, the expression "adequate evidence," as it is ordinarily interpreted, presupposes the concept of *knowledge*—knowledge, not of that for which we are said to *have* adequate evidence, but of something else. If a man says, for example, that we have adequate evidence for the hypothesis that no one can live on the planet Mercury, he is likely to mean that on the basis of what we know, there is very good reason to believe that no one can live on the planet Mercury. Or in slightly more technical language, he is saying that in relation to what is known, it is highly improbable that there can be life on Mercury.

We may say of this type of definition, then, what Socrates said of the attempt to define knowledge in terms of reason or explanation: "If, my boy, the command to add reason or explanation means learning to know and not merely getting an opinion . . . , our splendid definition of knowledge would be a fine affair! For learning to know is acquiring knowledge, is it not?" [*Theatetus* 209E]

Probability The concept of adequate evidence presupposes the concept of knowledge, but the concept of probability need not do so. May we say, then, that *probability* is that which, when added to true opinion, yields knowledge?

The term "probability," as it is ordinarily used, may be taken in a variety of senses. Of these, the most common are the *statistical* sense, the *inductive* sense, and the *absolute* sense. Whichever of these interpretations we adopt, we will find that the concept of probability does not provide us with the solution to Plato's problem.

(1) Taking the term in its statistical sense, we may say with Aristotle that the probable is "that which happens for the most part." Probability statements, when taken in this way, tell us something about the relative frequency with which a given property or event (say, death before the age of 100) occurs within a certain reference class or population (say, the class of men, or of philosophers, or of ancient Greek philosophers). Thus, the statement "It is highly probable that a given ancient Greek philosopher, for example, Anaxagoras, died before he reached 100," when taken in this way, will tell us that Anaxagoras was a member of a certain class of entities (ancient Greek philosophers), the vast majority of which died before they reached 100. Statistical probability statements, which may be arithmetically more complex, are analogous.

But just how are we to go about defining knowledge in terms of statistical probability? Let us allow ourselves to say that if a man believes something, then *what* he believes is a proposition. Then, we shall try to say something of this sort: If a man knows a given proposition to be true, then the proposition is a member of a certain wider class of propositions, the vast majority of which have a certain further property *P*. And we will hope to find a property *P* which is such that if a proposition is a member of a class of propositions, the vast majority of which have that property *P*, then the proposition is one that can be said to be *known* to be true—but *what* class of propositions, and what additional property *P*? It will not be enough to say that the class of propositions is the class of propositions that *S* believes and that *P* is the property of being true, for in this case we shall not have made any distinction between knowledge and true opinion. And it will be too much to say that the class is the class of true propositions that *S* believes and that the additional property *P* is the property of being *known* to be true, for in this case we will be presupposing the distinction we are trying to define.

(2) The *inductive* sense of "probable" may seem to be more promising. If, once again, we allow ourselves the term "proposition," then we may say that "probable," in its inductive sense, refers to a certain logical relation that holds between propositions.[1] Two propositions, *e* and *h*, may be so related logically that the proposition *h* may be said to be probable—that is, more probable than not—in relation to the proposition *e*. In such a case, *h* may be said to be *probable in relation to e*. If the reader can identify a good inductive argument, then he will have no trouble in identifying this relation. For to say that *h* is probable in relation to *e* is tantamount to saying that an argument having *e* as premise (*e* may be a conjunction of many propositions) and *h* as conclusion, would be a good inductive argument in favor of *h*. Let us say, for example, that "Anaxagoras lived to be 500 years old" is probable in relation to "Anaxagoras was an ancient Greek philosopher, and the vast majority of Greek philosophers lived to be 500 years old." The latter proposition, if we knew it to be true, would provide good inductive support for the former. Unfortunately, however, the question "What is a good inductive argument?" is at least as difficult as the question "What is the distinction between knowledge and true opinion?" And even if this were not so, inductive probability would not provide us with the answer to our question.

If we attempt to draw the distinction between knowledge and true opinion by reference to the inductive sense of "probable," then presumably we will say that our subject *S* knows the proposition *h* to be true, provided that *h* is probable in relation to a certain other proposition *e*. But *what* other proposition *e*? It will not be enough to say that there is a certain *true* proposition *e* which is such that *h* is probable on the basis of *e*, for in this case we will not be able to draw the distinction between knowledge and true opinion. We must say not only that *e* is true, but also that *e* has some further property as well. And what could this further property be—except that of being *known* by *S* to be

---

[1] The term "proposition" is a convenient abbreviatory device which we will use throughout the book. The relation between this term and the linguistic concept of a *sentence* and the metaphysical concept of a (possible) *state of affairs* will be touched upon in chaps. 5 and 7.

true? Hence, the problem of the *Theatetus* recurs, this time with respect to *e* instead of *h*. How are we to define "S knows that *e* is true"?

(3) When the term "probable" is used in the *absolute* sense, and this would seem to be its most frequent use, it is closely related to what is intended by the term "know." The phrase "in all probability" is often used to express the absolute sense of "probable." Thus, if we say "In all probability it will rain tomorrow," we mean that the hypothesis or proposition that it will rain tomorrow is more probable than not, in the inductive sense of "probable" just considered, in relation to those propositions that are *known* to be true or that could, very readily, be known to be true. We may be relating the hypothesis to what it is we happen to know ourselves; or we may be relating it to what it is we believe the experts happen to know (as we would be doing if we said "In all probability, a man will be landed on the moon before the century is over"); or we may be relating the hypothesis to the knowledge of some subclass of experts who are indicated by the context of utterance.

In its most straightforward sense, the concept of absolute probability might be defined in this way: A proposition *h* is *probable in the absolute sense* for a given subject *S*, provided that *h* is probable in the inductive sense, in relation to the conjunction of all those propositions that *S* knows to be true.[2] (Hence, we may equate what is expressed by "*h* is probable in the absolute sense for *S*" with what is expressed by "*S* has adequate evidence for *h*.") Since we must appeal to the concept of knowledge to explicate the concept of absolute probability, we cannot make use of the concept of absolute probability in order to complete our definition of knowledge.[3]

Observation   In writings on the philosophy of science, it is often assumed (1) that knowledge may be defined in terms of *observation* and (2) that observation, being a concept of physiology and psychology, can be defined in the terms of those sciences and without reference to knowledge. In support of the first contention, one might formulate the following definition: To say of someone *S* that *S* knows a certain prop-

---

[2] The following definition would achieve the same end without referring to "the conjunction of all those propositions that *S* knows to be true." A proposition *h* is probable in the absolute sense for *S* provided: there is a conjunction *e* of propositions that *S* knows to be true; *h* is probable in relation to *e*; and there is no proposition *i* such that both (1) *S* knows *i* to be true and (2) *h* is not probable in relation to the conjunction of *e* and *i*.

[3] The distinction between the inductive and statistical senses of "probable" is clearly drawn by Rudolf Carnap in *The Logical Foundations of Probability* (Chicago: University of Chicago Press, 1950). The expression "absolute probability," interpreted somewhat as here, was used by Bernard Bolzano in his *Wissenschaftslehre*, III (Leipzig: Felix Meiner, 1930), 267-68; this work was first published in 1837. Still another sense of "probable" is distinguished in footnote 17 of this chapter.

osition *h* to be true is to say that *S* has true opinion with respect to *h* and that *h* is an observation proposition for *S*. And in support of the second, one might point out that to say of a man that he observes a cat, for example, is to say that a cat is, for him, a stimulus object, that it has caused him to have a certain sensation, and perhaps also that it has "entered into his field of vision."

This approach to Plato's question will not serve to "bring the many sorts of knowledge under one definition," for as we shall see later in some detail, there are many sorts of knowledge that are not observational—for example, our knowledge of logic and mathematics and our knowledge of some of our own states of mind. But there is another difficulty that is even more serious.

The term "observation" is a member of a certain family of terms (compare "perceive," "see," "hear," "feel") each of which is subject to two quite different types of interpretation. If we interpret any one of these terms in such a way that, on that interpretation, one of the two contentions comprising the present suggestion will be true (and we may do this), then, on that interpretation of the term, the other contention will be false.

We may say of a man simply that he observes a cat on the roof. Or we may say of him that he observes *that* a cat is on the roof. In the second case, the verb "observe" takes a "that"-clause, a propositional clause, as its grammatical object. We may distinguish, therefore, between a "propositional" and a "nonpropositional" use of the term "observe," and we may make an analogous distinction for "perceive," "see," "hear," and "feel."

If we take the verb "observe" propositionally, saying of the man that he observes that a cat is on the roof, or that he observes a cat to be on the roof, then we may also say of him that he *knows* that a cat is on the roof; for in the propositional sense of "observe," observation may be said to imply knowledge. But if we take the verb nonpropositionally, saying of the man only that he observes a cat which is on the roof, then what we say will not imply that he knows that there is a cat on the roof. For a man may be said to observe a cat, to see a cat, or hear a cat, in the nonpropositional sense of these terms, without his knowing that a cat is what it is that he is observing, or seeing, or hearing. "It wasn't until the following day that I found out that what I saw was only a cat."

The distinction between these two senses of "observe" and the other related terms may also be illustrated by the following passage in *Robinson Crusoe*: "When, one morning the day broke, and all unexpectedly before their eyes a ship stood, what it was was evident at a glance to Crusoe. . . . But how was it with Friday? As younger and uncivilized, his eyes were presumably better than those of his master.

That is, Friday saw the ship really the best of the two; and yet he could hardly be said to see it at all." Using "see" nonpropositionally, we may say that Friday not only saw the ship, but saw it better than Crusoe did; using it propositionally, we may say that Crusoe, but not Friday, saw *that* it was a ship and hence, that Friday hardly saw a ship at all.

We can define the Friday, nonpropositional sense of "observe" by means of the terms of psychology and physiology. But this sense of observation does not imply knowledge, and we cannot use it to complete our definition of knowledge. We must appeal instead to the Crusoe, propositional sense of "observe." What, then, did Crusoe have that Friday did not have?

The obvious answer is that Crusoe had *knowledge*. His senses enabled him to *know*, with the result that "what it was was evident at a glance." This sense of "observation," therefore, must be defined in terms of knowledge, and so we are left, once again, with Plato's problem.

Knowledge as an ethical concept   If we are to solve the problem, we must find a definition of *knowledge* that is not patently circular. We cannot be content to define knowledge by reference, say, to "that which falls within our cognizance." Nor will it do merely to introduce some technical term and then resolve to use it in the way in which we ordinarily use the word "knowledge." We may say, if we like, that to constitute knowledge, a true opinion must also be one that is "evident," but we must not suppose that the introduction of the technical term is itself sufficient to throw any light upon our problem.

Let us consider, then, the possibility of defining knowledge in ethical terms. To know that *h* is true will be not only to have true opinion with respect to *h*, but also to have a certain right or duty with respect to *h*. Whether such a definition will turn out to be circular will depend upon how we specify the right or duty in question. The terms "right" and "duty" are not technical terms invented merely in order to complete our definition. We may assume that "right" and "duty" are correlative terms: A man has a right to perform a certain act A if, and only if, it is not his duty to refrain from performing A, and he has a duty to perform A if, and only if, he does not have the right to refrain from performing A. Instead of saying "He has a duty to perform A," we may also say "He ought to perform A."

One may object that any such definition would throw no light upon the concept of knowledge, for what it is to have a right or a duty is at least as obscure as what it is to know. The obvious reply is: The philosopher is indeed confronted not only with the difficult concept of knowledge, but also with the difficult concept of a right or a duty; but if he can succeed in defining one of these by reference to the other, then he will have progressed at least to the extent of finding himself with one difficult concept, where formerly he had found himself with two.[4]

What right or duty, then, does the knower have with respect to that which he knows? A simple answer would be: If a man knows that a certain proposition is true, then he has the duty to accept or believe that proposition. More exactly, S knows that h is true, provided that (1) S accepts or believes h; (2) h is true; and (3) S has the duty to accept or believe h. Would this be an adequate definition?

The term "duty" must be taken in its ordinary sense if the definition is to be of any significance. But "duty," as we ordinarily understand the term, is used in connection with actions, or possible actions, that are within the agent's power and for which he can be held responsible if he performs them. ("'Ought' implies 'can.'") But are beliefs actions, or possible actions, that are within anyone's power?[5] And can a man be held responsible for what he believes, or fails to believe? (We often speak of what a man ought to know, but seldom, if ever, of what a man ought to believe.)

There is a difficulty that is even more serious: If beliefs—more exactly, believings—are actions for which we can be held responsible, then the proposed definition would imply that to turn a man's true opinion into knowledge, it would be sufficient to make the holding of that opinion a duty. But it is at least conceivable that a man may have the duty to accept a true proposition which he does not know to be true. For example, a man may have the duty to believe that the members of his family are honest or faithful without in fact knowing that they are. Or a sick man, who has various unfulfilled obligations, may have the duty to accept certain propositions if, by accepting them, he

[4] Thus, some moral philosophers have attempted to define "duty" in terms of "know"—e.g., in terms of what an "ideal observer" would approve if only he knew all of the relevant facts. See Francis Hutcheson, *An Essay on the Nature and Conduct of the Passions, with Illustrations upon the Moral Sense* (1728); see also, Roderick Firth, "Ethical Absolutism and the Ideal Observer," *Philosophy and Phenomenological Research*, XII (1952), 317-45. This way of defining "duty," however, involves difficulties analogous to those encountered in trying to define "know." If the characteristics that would make an observer "ideal" include certain moral qualifications, then an "ideal-observer" definition of "duty" may become circular; and if they do not, then it may be impossible to determine what such an observer would approve, in which case the definition would be inapplicable.

[5] Descartes assumed that beliefs are acts which are within our power, and Spinoza, that they are not. This general problem is discussed in: C. S. Peirce, *Collected Papers*, ed. Charles Hartshorne and Paul Weiss, I (Cambridge: Harvard University Press, 1931), 331-34; H. H. Price, "Belief and Will," *Aristotelian Society Supplementary Volume*, XXVIII (1954), 1-26; C. I. Lewis, *The Ground and Nature of the Right*, "Right Believing and Right Concluding" (New York: Columbia University Press, 1955), Chap. 2; and Stuart Hampshire, *Thought and Action* (New York: The Viking Press, Inc., 1959), Chap. 2.

can make himself well and useful once again. The proposed definition would have the consequence that, if these duties to believe are fulfilled, and if the propositions thus believed happen to be true, then the believer, *ipso facto*, knows that they are true. And this is absurd.[6]

Analogous considerations hold if we define knowing in terms of "the right to believe," instead of "the duty to believe."

Let us consider, then, another type of right or duty, one that is more closely related to the concept of knowing—the right or duty that we have, in certain cases, to take precautions. Taking precautions is a kind of activity. When a man takes precautions, he prepares for the worst, even though he may not expect it to happen. For example, he may not believe that his house will burn, but he takes precautions by buying fire insurance. But if he *knows* that a given proposition is true, then, it would seem, there is no point in his taking any precautions against the possibility that the proposition is false. If, somehow, he knew that his house would never burn, then, it would seem, there would be no point in his insuring the house against fire or otherwise taking precautions against the possibility that his house might burn. Suppose, then, we say that a man knows *h* to be true, provided that no matter what he may do, he has the right to rely upon *h*—that is to say, no matter what he may do, he does not have the duty to take precautions against the possibility that *h* is false.

This definition has been suggested by a familiar doctrine of scholastic philosophy: If a man *knows*, then he need have no "fear of error," and so far as what is known is concerned, his intellect may be in "a state of repose." [7] A. J. Ayer has suggested a similar definition, saying that the man who knows, as contrasted with the man who merely has true opinion, is the man who has the "right to be sure." [8]

But here, too, there are difficulties. The duty to take precautions in any particular case is a function not only of what is known, but also of what happens to be at stake—if not, indeed, of what is *known* to be at stake. Where the stakes are small, there may be no need to take precautions—whether or not one knows. And where the stakes are large, there may be a duty to take precautions—whether or not one knows. Moreover, the duty to take precautions may arise in still other ways. Even if a captain knows that his ship is seaworthy, he may yet have

[6] See Roderick Firth, "Chisholm and the Ethics of Belief," *Philosophical Review*, LXVIII (1959), 493-506.

[7] See D. J. Mercier, *Critériologie générale, ou Théorie générale de la certitude*, 8th ed. (Paris: Felix Alcan, 1923), pp. 420-21; P. Coffey, *Epistemology, or the Theory of Knowledge*, I (London: Longmans, Green & Company, Ltd., 1917), 54-55.

[8] *The Problem of Knowledge* (New York: St. Martin's Press, Inc., 1955), pp. 31-35.

the obligation to provide lifeboats and to take other precautions against the possibility that it is not. For he may have the obligation to reassure his passengers; or he may have sworn to obey the law and thus have acquired the obligation to take precautions with every sailing.

Again, there are circumstances under which a man may be said to have the duty to rely upon certain propositions about his friends, or upon certain propositions that his friends have assured him are true, even though he does not know these propositions to be true. One of the duties of the Christian, for example, is said to be that of faith— where faith is a matter of trust, a matter of relying upon the several tenets that make up the doctrine of Christianity. The virtue of having faith is thought by some Christians to lie in the very fact that the tenets of the faith are propositions which are *not* known to be true and which, indeed, are extremely unreasonable.[9] If it is the duty of the Christian to have faith, and if the tenets of that faith happen to be true, then, according to the proposed definition of knowledge, it will follow from these facts alone that the Christian *knows* these tenets to be true.

It is not enough, then, to define "S knows that *h* is true" by reference merely to the right not to take precautions against the possibility that *h* is false. For S may know that *h* is true and yet not have this right; or he may have the right (for he may have the duty, and if he has the duty he has the right) and yet not know that *h* is true.

By introducing proper qualifications, we could conceivably formulate an ethical definition of "know" that would not be subject to such difficulties. But no one has yet been able to formulate satisfactorily just what the qualifications are that are needed. At the present time, then, we do not have an ethical definition that will constitute a solution to the problem of the *Theatetus*.[10]

---

[9] Cf. the following passage from Kierkegaard's *Concluding Unscientific Postscript*: "Suppose a man who wishes to acquire faith; let the comedy begin. He wishes to have faith, but he wishes also to safeguard himself by means of an objective inquiry and its approximation process. What happens? With the help of the approximation process the absurd becomes something different: it becomes probable, it becomes increasingly probable, it becomes extremely and emphatically probable. Now he is ready to believe it, and he ventures to claim for himself that he does not believe as shoemakers and tailors and simple folk believe, but only after long deliberation. Now he is ready to believe it [i.e., to accept it on faith]; and lo, now it has become precisely impossible to believe it. Anything that is almost probable, is something he can almost know, or as good as know, or extremely and emphatically almost know —but it is impossible to *believe*. For the absurd is the object of faith, and the only object that can be believed." From *A Kierkegaard Anthology*, ed. Robert Bretall (Princeton: Princeton University Press, 1947), pp. 220-21.

[10] Still other difficulties are noted by Herbert Heidelberger in, "On Defining Epistemic Expressions," *Journal of Philosophy*, LX (1963), 344-48.

It may well be asked, at this point, whether our problem has not been misconceived—whether what we take to be a problem may not actually rest upon a false presupposition. We have been supposing all along that there is something x such that, when x is added to true opinion, the result is knowledge, and we have sought, so far in vain, for this something x. But is it necessary to make any such supposition in order to make the distinction between knowledge and true opinion?

There are those who believe that if we note certain ways in which people use the *word* "know," we will then be able to see that the supposition in question is mistaken. One source of this belief is an influential paper by J. L. Austin, in which he describes what he calls the "performative" function of "I know." [11]

The concept of a "performative" function may be illustrated by referring to the ordinary use of the expression "I promise." Usually, when a man utters the words "I promise," the point of his utterance is not to report anything; the man's concern is to make the promise, not to describe himself as making a promise. To utter the words "I promise," under ordinary conditions, is to promise. "I request" is similar. Thus, if a man uses the word "request" in the third person, saying "He requests," then he is describing or reporting what some other person is doing; or if he uses the word in the first person, but in the past tense, saying "I requested," then he is describing or reporting something that he himself was doing; but if he uses the word in the first person and in the present tense, saying "I request," then his point is not to report or describe himself as requesting—his point is to make a request. The same thing holds for such verbs as "order," "warn," "guarantee," and "baptize." (One indication of a performative use, Austin remarks, is the fact that "the little word 'hereby' actually occurs or might naturally be inserted"—as in "Trespassers are hereby warned that cars will be towed away at owner's expense.")

The expression "I know," Austin points out, performs a function very similar to that of "I promise." When a man utters the words "I promise" he provides a guarantee; he stakes his reputation and binds himself to others—and similarly, for saying "I know." Saying "I know," Austin writes, "is *not* saying 'I have performed a specially striking feat of cognition, superior, in the same scale as believing and being sure, even to being merely quite sure': for there *is* nothing in that scale superior to being quite sure. Just as promising is not something superior,

[11] "Other Minds," *Proceedings of the Aristotelian Society*, Supplementary Volume XX (1946); reprinted in Austin's *Philosophical Papers*, ed. J. O. Urmson and G. J. Warnock (New York: Oxford University Press, 1961), pp. 44-84.

in the same scale as hoping and intending, even to merely fully intend-ing: for there *is* nothing in that scale superior to fully intending. When I say 'I know,' I *give others my word: I give others my authority* for saying that 'S is P.' " [12] And Austin concludes: "To suppose 'I know' is a descriptive phrase, is only one example of the *descriptive fallacy*, so common in philosophy." [13]

It is in the spirit of these observations also to note that where "I know" performs the function of giving assurance, "I believe" may per-form that of taking it away. For to say "I believe," under certain cir-cumstances, is tantamount to saying "Don't take *my* word for it—I won't be responsible." How, then, could "knowing" ever be thought to imply "believing"—if the function of the one is to give, and that of the other, to take away?

On the basis of such considerations, some philosophers have con-cluded that the problem of the *Theatetus* is a pseudo-problem. It is said to be a pseudo-problem because it is thought to be based upon a false assumption, the assumption, namely, that there *is* a state which may be described or reported by means of the word "know." And it is by committing the "descriptive fallacy" that one is led to make this assumption.

But let us look more carefully at the concept of a "performative utterance."

Almost every utterance may be said to be performative in at least one respect, for almost every utterance is intended to have effects other than those of simply describing or reporting. What, then, is the pecu-liarity of the particular expressions that Austin calls "performative"? Austin did not provide a clear definition of the concept, but I think that "performative utterances" might be described as follows.

There are certain acts—e.g., requesting, ordering, guaranteeing, baptizing—which have this characteristic: When the circumstances are right, then to perform the act it is enough to make an utterance con-taining words which the speaker commonly uses to designate such an act. A standard way of making a request, among English-speaking peo-ple, is to make an utterance beginning with "I request" (the same thing holds for promising, ordering, guaranteeing, baptizing). Let us say, then, of anyone who performs an act in this way, that his utterance is a "performative utterance"—in what we may call the strict sense of this term.

An utterance beginning with "I want" is not performative in this strict sense, for it cannot be said to be an "act" of wanting. But "I want"

---

[12] *Philosophical Papers*, p. 67. Cf. C. S. Peirce, *Collected Papers*, V (1932), 383-87.
[13] *Ibid.*, p. 71.

is often used to accomplish what one might accomplish by means of the strict performative "I request." Let us say, then, that "I want" may be a "performative utterance" in an *extended* sense of the latter expression.

In which of these senses may an utterance of "I know" be said to be performative? Clearly, "I know" is not performative in what I have called the strict sense of the term, for knowing is not an "act" that can be performed by saying "I know." To say "I *promise* that *p*," at least under certain circumstances, *is* to promise that *p*; but to say "I know that *p*" is not itself to know that *p*. (One may say "I hereby promise," but not "I hereby know.") "I know" is related to "I guarantee" and "I give you my word" in the way in which "I want" is related to "I request." For "I know" is often used to accomplish what one may accomplish by the strict performative "I guarantee" or "I give you my word." Hence, "I know" may be performative in an extended sense of the term.

"I want" is not always a substitute for "I request." I may tell you what I want, and thus, describe my psychological state, even when I know there is no possibility of your helping me in getting what I want. And "I know" is not always a substitute for "I guarantee." I may tell you—confess or boast to you—that I know some of the things that you also know, and on an occasion when you neither need nor want my guarantee. ("I believe," similarly, is not always a substitute for "I can't provide you with any guarantees," for I may tell you what I believe on occasion when I *am* prepared to give you guarantees.)

What, then, of Austin's remark "To suppose 'I know' is a descriptive phrase, is only one example of the *descriptive fallacy*, so common in philosophy"? It looks very much as though Austin was assuming mistakenly that "I know" is performative in the strict sense and not merely in the extended sense. Yet, just as an utterance of "I want" may serve *both* to say something about me and to get you to do something, an utterance of "I know" may serve both to say something about me and to provide you with guarantees. To suppose that the performance of the nondescriptive function is inconsistent with a simultaneous performance of the descriptive function might be called, therefore, an example of the *performative fallacy*.

The expression "I know" is not to be taken lightly, and therefore, if we are philosophers, we may ask what the conditions are that entitle one to say it. Thus, Austin says: "If you say you *know* something, the most immediate challenge takes the form of asking 'Are you in a position to know?': that is, you must undertake to show, not merely that you are sure of it, but that it is *within your cognizance*." [14]

If a man is entitled to say "I know that *h*," it may well be that he

---

[14] *Philosophical Papers*, p. 68. I have italicized the final three words.

has performed no striking feat of cognition, but *h* does "fall within his cognizance." And if *h* does thus fall within his cognizance, then surely, whether or not he *says* "I know," he *does* know. ("He knows but he isn't saying.") Hence, it would seem there *is* a state, after all, that may be described or reported by means of the word "know." [15] It is by committing the "performative fallacy" that one is led to suppose that there is not.

Other
epistemic
terms

"Know" is one of a family of terms—we might call them terms of epistemic appraisal—which present us with essentially similar problems. We can throw some light upon "know" by noting its relations to other members of the same family.

Just as we may say of a man that he *knows* a certain hypothesis or proposition to be true, we may also say: a certain hypothesis is *evident* to him; it is *reasonable* of him to accept a certain hypothesis; one hypothesis is, for him, *more reasonable* than another; a certain hypothesis is for him *gratuitous*, or *indifferent*, or *acceptable*, or *unacceptable*.

If we say that a certain hypothesis or proposition is "unacceptable," where "unacceptable" is to be taken as a term of epistemic appraisal, we mean not that the proposition is incapable of being accepted, but rather, that epistemically it is unworthy of being accepted. The negation of any proposition that a man knows to be true, or of any proposition that is evident to him, could be said to be a proposition that is, for him, unacceptable. Hence, for most of us, "Chicago is not on Lake Michigan" would be unacceptable. Other propositions may be unacceptable even though their negations are not evident or not known to be true. For there are some propositions which are such that both they and their negations are unacceptable. These are the propositions which, in the terms of the ancient sceptics, any reasonable man would *withhold*; he would neither believe them nor disbelieve them, neither affirm them nor deny them. Obvious examples of such propositions are those that generate paradox, e.g., Russell's "The class of all classes that are not members of themselves is a member of itself." According to the rigid ethics of belief advocated by W. K. Clifford, every proposition for

---

[15] J. O. Urmson proposed an account of the use of "I know" similar to Austin's and then attempted to extend the account to second and third persons and to other tenses in the following way: To say, for example, that Mr. Jones *knew* some proposition to be true is to say that Mr. Jones was "in a position in which he was entitled to say 'I know.'" And what is it to be "in a position in which one is entitled to say 'I know'"? According to Urmson, it is to be in the position of having "all the *evidence* one could need"—which brings us back to the point at which we began our discussion of Plato's problem. See "Parenthetical Verbs," in *Essays in Conceptual Analysis*, ed. A. G. N. Flew (New York: St. Martin's Press, Inc., 1956), p. 199; the italics are mine.

which there is "insufficient evidence" is also unacceptable.[16] According to positivistic philosophers, some propositions that are unverifiable and all propositions that have a metaphysical subject matter may also be said to be unacceptable.

A "gratuitous" proposition may be described as one which there is no point in accepting. If we could say that an unacceptable proposition is one that ought not to be accepted, then we could say that a gratuitous proposition is one that need not be accepted. Hence, the charge of gratuitousness is less serious than that of unacceptability: Every unacceptable proposition is gratuitous, but some gratuitous propositions (unless Clifford is right) are not unacceptable. The astronomy of Copernicus, according to some, makes that of Ptolemy gratuitous, but it does not make it unacceptable. The Ptolemaic astronomy is not unacceptable, but since it is needlessly complex, it is gratuitous.

Sometimes propositions are said to be epistemically "indifferent," but we must distinguish two quite different uses of this term. (1) Will it rain in Baltimore a year from today? For most of us, the proposition is epistemically "indifferent" in that there is as much, or as little, reason for believing it as there is for disbelieving it. Any proposition that has a probability of .5 in relation to everything that is known could be said to be indifferent in this first sense of the term. (2) An act is said to be morally indifferent if performance of the act is permissible and if non-performance is also permissible. It is sometimes said analogously that a proposition is epistemically indifferent if the proposition is acceptable and if its negation is also acceptable.

If a proposition is indifferent in the first of these two senses of the term, then it is not indifferent in the second. For if there is no ground for choosing between the proposition and its negation, then suspension of belief would seem to be the reasonable course, in which case neither the proposition nor its negation would be acceptable. It may well be, in fact, that no proposition is indifferent in the second sense of the term.

Some propositions are "beyond reasonable doubt." Or as we may also say, they are such that it is "reasonable" for a man to believe them. These include those propositions for which he has adequate evidence (in the sense of "adequate evidence" discussed earlier). For presumably, it is reasonable for a man to believe any proposition that is more probable than not in relation to the totality of what he knows. (This is the epistemic thesis that is sometimes expressed by saying "induction is

---

[16] See "The Ethics of Belief," in *Lectures and Essays*, II (London: Macmillan & Co., Ltd., 1879), 163-205.

justified." [17]) An important epistemological question (to be discussed in Chapter 3) concerns whether or not there are any *other* propositions which it is reasonable for a man to accept.

Some propositions are "evident" as well as reasonable. Any proposition that a man knows to be true is one that may be said to be evident for him. But it may be that some propositions that are evident for him are not propositions that he knows to be true. Thus, it has been held that whatever is logically entailed by what is evident, is itself evident. But some of the propositions that are logically entailed by what a man knows may be such that he does not know that they are entailed by what he knows, and they may even be propositions which he does not accept (he may know that all philosophers are men and yet refrain from believing that everything that is not a man is something that is not a philosopher). In this case, he will refrain from accepting or believing certain propositions which are evident for him; and an evident proposition that is not accepted cannot be said to be a proposition that is known. Again, any proposition that is both evident and false would be a proposition that is evident but not known; whether there are any such propositions is an extraordinarily difficult question to which we shall return.

Hence, there are important differences between saying that a certain proposition is "evident" for a man and saying that he has "adequate evidence" for that proposition. We may note three such differences: (1) A man may have adequate evidence for a proposition that is not evident to him. If he happens to know, for example, that there are 1,000 balls in the urn and that 999 of them are red, and if he knows further that one of them will be drawn at random, then he might be said to have adequate evidence for the proposition that the ball to be drawn will be red; but before the ball is drawn it will not be evident for him that it is red. (2) The "logic" of the concept of the evident differs from that of the concept of adequate evidence. Thus, if the balls in the urn are to be taken out one at a time, and none of them returned, perhaps we may say that the man now has adequate evidence, with respect to

---

[17] We have been using "*h* is probable for *S*," in its *absolute* sense, to mean that *h* is inductively supported by (is more probable than not in relation to) what is known by *S*. But sometimes the expression is used *epistemically* to mean merely that *h* is a proposition which it is reasonable for *S* to accept. This ambiguity seems to have misled some philosophers into supposing that they can easily demonstrate the justifiability of induction. Taking "probable" in its epistemic sense, they note that a probable proposition is one that is reasonable; then, taking "probable" in its *absolute* sense, they note that a probable proposition is one that is inductively supported by what is known; and finally, by committing the fallacy of equivocation, they deduce that if a proposition is inductively supported by what is known, then it is one that it is reasonable to accept.

each particular drawing, that the ball drawn on that particular occasion will be red, but he does not have adequate evidence for the proposition that, on every occasion, the ball that is drawn will be red. But if, somehow, it were *evident* for him, with respect to *each* occasion, that on that occasion a red ball would be drawn, then it would also be evident for him that on *every* occasion a red ball would be drawn. (3) There may be propositions that are evident for a man, but which are such that he cannot properly be said to *have* adequate evidence for them. For if we follow ordinary usage, we will say of such propositions as "I seem to remember having been in this place before," that they are propositions which may *be* evident for a man at a given time, but not that they are propositions for which he *has* evidence at that time. Thus, if I *have* evidence for a given proposition, then I will be able to cite certain *other* propositions as being my evidence for that proposition; but even though it is evident for me that I seem to remember having been in this place before, there are no other propositions I could cite as being my *evidence* for the proposition that I seem to remember having been in this place before.[18]

Some definitions   If "know" and the other epistemic terms we have been discussing can all be defined in terms of one epistemic term or locution, then perhaps it can be said that we have provided a partial solution to Plato's problem.

Let us remind ourselves, first, that we may take one of three different attitudes toward any given proposition: we may believe or accept the proposition; we may disbelieve or reject the proposition (and this is the same as believing or accepting the negation of the proposition); or we may "withhold" the proposition—that is, we may refrain from believing it and we may also refrain from disbelieving it. And secondly, let us remind ourselves that for any proposition and any person, some of these attitudes will be *more reasonable*, at any given time, than others. Thus, St. Augustine suggested that even though there might be ground to question the reliability of the senses, it would be more reasonable for most of us most of the time to believe that we could rely upon them than to believe that we could not. Presumably, for most of us at the present time, it is more reasonable to withhold the proposition that there is life on Venus than it is to accept it; but it is more reasonable to accept the proposition that there is life on Venus than it is to accept the proposition that there is life on Mercury. What is suggested when we say of one of these attitudes that it is more reasonable than another, is this: If the person in question were a rational being, if his

[18] For further discussion of some of these points, cf. Herbert Heidelberger, "Knowledge, Certainty, and Probability," *Inquiry,* VI (1963), 242-50.

concerns were purely intellectual, and if he were to choose between the two attitudes, then he would choose the more reasonable in preference to the less reasonable.[19]

By reference to this concept of one epistemic attitude being more reasonable than another for a given subject at a given time, we can define and systematize our various epistemic concepts. A proposition is *reasonable* or "beyond reasonable doubt," if believing it is more reasonable than withholding it; it is *gratuitous* if believing it is not more reasonable than withholding it; it is *unacceptable* if withholding it is more reasonable than believing it; and it is *acceptable* if withholding it is not more reasonable than believing it.[20] And a proposition *h* may be said to be *evident* for a subject *S* provided (1) that *h* is reasonable for *S* and (2) that there is no proposition *i* such that it is more reasonable for *S* to believe *i* than it is for him to believe *h*. We thus have a hierarchy of epistemic terms: Every proposition that is evident is reasonable, but not conversely; and every proposition that is reasonable is acceptable, but not conversely.[21] We shall see the importance of such a hierarchy in Chapter 3, where we discuss the problem of formulating a theory of empirical evidence.

Having defined the evident, we may now return to the problem of the *Theatetus* and to the definition with which we began.

[19] The following observation by William James reminds us that such a person—a rational being whose concerns are purely intellectual—would not be motivated merely by the desire to play it safe. "There are two ways of looking at our duty in the matter of opinion,—ways entirely different, and yet ways about whose difference the theory of knowledge seems hitherto to have shown very little concern. We *must know the truth*: and *we must avoid error*,—these are our first and great commandments as would-be knowers; but they are not two ways of stating an identical commandment, they are two separable laws. . . . By choosing between them we may end by coloring differently our whole intellectual life. . . . For my part, I can believe that worse things than being duped may happen to a man." From *The Will to Believe and Other Essays in Popular Philosophy* (New York: David McKay Co. Inc., 1911), pp. 17-19.

[20] Of the two senses of "indifferent" distinguished above, a proposition could be said to be *indifferent*, in the first sense, if believing it is not more reasonable than disbelieving it and if disbelieving it is not more reasonable than believing it. It would be indifferent, in the second sense, if both it and its negation were acceptable; but as we have noted, there is ground for questioning whether any proposition is indifferent in this second sense.

[21] An "epistemic logic," exhibiting the logical relations among these concepts, could be developed on the basis of these three assumptions: (1) If one attitude is more reasonable than another and the other more reasonable than a third, then the first is more reasonable than the third. (2) If one attitude is more reasonable than another, then the other is not more reasonable than it. (3) If withholding a given proposition is not more reasonable than believing it, then believing it is more reasonable than disbelieving it (e.g., if agnosticism is not more reasonable than theism, then theism is more reasonable than atheism).

S knows at t that h is true, provided: (1) S believes h at t; (2) h is true; and (3) h is evident at t for S.[22]

We thus have a partial solution to the problem. We have defined "know" in terms of "evident." And we have defined "evident" in terms of "more reasonable." The definition of "evident" is not completely empty, for we have seen that "more reasonable" is also adequate for the definition of other basic terms of epistemic appraisal. Our definition, therefore, enables us to see the ways in which these various concepts are related. We may leave unanswered the important question of whether it is possible to define "more reasonable" in strictly ethical terms.

What propositions, then, can be said to be evident?

[22] If we countenance the possibility that some propositions are both evident and false, we must add a qualification to the definition in order to remove a difficulty pointed out by Edmund L. Gettier in "Is Justified True Belief Knowledge?" *Analysis*, XXV (1963), 121-23. Suppose "I see a sheep in the field" is a false proposition *i* that is evident for S (he mistakes a dog for a sheep); then "A sheep is in the field" (*h*) will also be evident for S. Suppose further that there happens to be a sheep in the field that S does not see. This situation, obviously, would not warrant our saying S *knows* that there is a sheep in the field; yet it satisfies the conditions of our definition, for S believes *h*, *h* is true, and *h* is evident for S. To rule out this type of situation, it would be necessary to add a qualification to our definition of "know."

Let us say that a proposition *e* "justifies" a proposition *h* provided *e* and *h* are such that, for any subject and any time, if *e* is evident to that subject at that time then *h* is evident to that subject at that time; and let us say that a "basic proposition" is an evident proposition such that the only evident propositions that thus justify it are propositions that entail it. To meet the difficulty, we might consider adding the following clause which would make our definition of "know" recursive:

"Either (1) *h* is a basic proposition for S at *t*, or (2) *h* is entailed by a set of propositions that are known by S at *t*, or (3) a proposition that is known by S at *t* and that does not justify any false proposition justifies *h*."

In Chap. 2 we will consider propositions that are "basic" in the sense defined, and in Chap. 3 we will consider cases in which a proposition may thus "justify" a proposition that it does not entail. If it is necessary to add such a fourth clause to our definition of "know," then *knowing that one knows*, i.e., being certain, is considerably more difficult than merely knowing. For discussions of this latter question, see Jaakko Hintikka, *Knowledge and Belief* (Ithaca: Cornell University Press, 1962), Chap. 5, and Roderick M. Chisholm, "The Logic of Knowing," *Journal of Philosophy*, LX (1963), 775-95.

THE DIRECTLY EVIDENT

2

Socratic
questions In order to formulate, or make explicit, our rules of evidence, we
will do well to proceed as we do in logic, when formulating rules of
inference, or in moral philosophy, when formulating rules of action.
We suppose that we have at our disposal certain instances which the
rules should countenance or permit and other instances which the rules
should reject or forbid; and we suppose that by investigating these instances we can formulate criteria which any instance must satisfy if it
is to be accepted or permitted, as well as criteria which any instance must
satisfy if it is to be rejected or forbidden.[1] To obtain the instances we
need if we are to formulate rules of evidence, we may proceed in the
following way.

We consider certain things that we know to be true, or think we
know to be true, or certain things which, upon reflection, we would be
willing to call *evident*. With respect to each of these, we then try to
formulate a reasonable answer to the question "What justification do
you have for thinking you know this thing to be true?" or "What justification do you have for counting this thing as something that is evident?" In beginning with what we think we know to be true, or with
what, after reflection, we would be willing to count as being evident, we

[1] "The nature of the good can be learned from experience only if the content of
experience be first classified into good and bad, or grades of better and worse. Such
classification or grading already involves the legislative application of the same
principle which is sought. In logic, principles can be elicited by generalization from
examples only if cases of valid reasoning have first been segregated by some criterion.
In esthetics, the laws of the beautiful may be derived from experience only if the
criteria of beauty have first been correctly applied." C. I. Lewis, *Mind and the
World-Order* (New York: Charles Scribner's Sons, 1929), p. 29; cf. his discussion
of the "critique of cogency," in *The Ground and Nature of the Right* (New York:
Columbia University Press, 1955), pp. 20-38.

are assuming that the truth we are seeking is "already implicit in the mind which seeks it, and needs only to be elicited and brought to clear reflection." [2] Whether we are justified in beginning in this way will be discussed in Chapter 4.

There are philosophers who point out, with respect to some things that are quite obviously known to be true, that questions concerning their justification "do not arise," for (they say) to express a doubt concerning such things is to "violate the rules of our language." But these objections do not apply to the type of question that we are discussing here; for these questions need not be taken to express any doubts, or to indicate any attitude of scepticism. Designed only to elicit information, the questions are not challenges and they do not imply or presuppose that there is any ground for doubting, or for suspecting, that to which they pertain.[3] When Aristotle considered an invalid mood and asked himself "What is wrong with this?" he was trying to learn; he need not have been suggesting to himself that perhaps nothing was wrong with the mood.

It should also be noted that when we ask ourselves, concerning what we may think we know to be true, "What justification do I have for counting this as something that is evident?" or "What justification do I have for thinking I know that this is something that is true?" we are not asking any of the following questions: "What further evidence can I find in support of this?" "How did I come to believe this or find out that it is true?" "How would I go about persuading some other reasonable person that it is true?" We must not expect, therefore, that answers to these latter questions will be, *ipso facto*, answers to the questions that we are asking. Our questions are Socratic and therefore not at all of the type that one ordinarily asks.[4]

---

[2] *Mind and the World-Order*, p. 19.

[3] These remarks also apply to Leonard Nelson's statement "If one asks whether one possesses objectively valid cognitions at all, one thereby presupposes that the objectivity of cognition is questionable at first . . .''; *Socratic Method and Critical Philosophy* (New Haven: Yale University Press, 1949), p. 190. One of the unfortunate consequences of the work of Descartes and, in the present century, the work of Bertrand Russell and Edmund Husserl, is the widely accepted supposition that questions about the justification for counting evident statements *as* evident must be challenges or expressions of doubts. See Bertrand Russell's *Problems of Philosophy* (New York: Holt, Rinehart & Winston, Inc., 1912) and his many other writings on the theory of knowledge, and E. Husserl's *Méditations Cartésiennes* (Paris: J. Vrin, 1931), also published as *Cartesianische Meditationen und Pariser Vorträge* (The Hague: Martinus Nijhoff, 1950). The objections to this approach to the concept of the evident were clearly put forth by A. Meinong; see his *Gesammelte Abhandlungen*, II (Leipzig: Johann Ambrosius Barth, 1913), 191.

[4] According to Xenophon, Charicles said to Socrates: "You generally ask questions when you know quite well how the matter stands; these are the questions you are not to ask." [*Memorabilia*, I, 2, 36]

In many instances the answers to our questions will take the following form:

What justifies me in counting it as evident (in thinking that I know) that *a* is *F*, is the fact that (1) it is evident that *b* is *G* and (2) if it is evident that *b* is *G* then it is evident that *a* is *F*.

For example: "What justifies me in counting it as evident that he has that disorder is the fact that it is evident that he has those symptoms, and if it is evident that he has those symptoms, then it is evident that he has that disorder." Such an answer has two parts. First, we say that our justification for counting one thing as evident is the fact that something else is evident. And secondly, we offer what may be called a "rule of evidence": We make a statement which says that if certain conditions obtain, then something may be said to be evident. One could say of such a rule that it tells us that one thing *confers evidence* upon another.

This type of answer to our Socratic questions shifts the burden of justification from one claim to another. For we may now ask, "What justifies me in counting it as evident that *b* is *G*?" or "What justifies me in thinking I know that *b* is *G*?" And possibly we will formulate, once again, an answer of the first sort: "What justifies me in counting it as evident that *b* is *G* is the fact that (1) it is evident that *c* is *H* and (2) if it is evident that *c* is *H*, then it is evident that *b* is *G*." ("What justifies me in counting it as evident that he has those symptoms is the fact that it is evident that his temperature is recorded as being high. . . .") How long can we continue in this way?

Conceivably, we might continue *ad indefinitum*, justifying each new claim that we elicit by still another claim. Or we might complete a vicious circle: Having justified "*a* is *F*" by appeal to "*b* is *G*" and "*b* is *G*" by reference to "*c* is *H*," we might then justify "*c* is *H*" by reference to "*a* is *F*." Actually, we will do neither of these; we will find that our Socratic questions lead us to a proper stopping place. But how are we to recognize it?

Sextus Empiricus remarked that every object of apprehension seems to be apprehended either through itself or through another object.[5] Those things, if there are any, that are "apprehended through themselves" might provide us with a stopping place. But what could they be? The form of our Socratic questions suggests a way of finding an answer. Let us say provisionally that we have found a proper stopping place when the answer to our question may take the following form:

What justifies me in counting it as evident that *a* is *F* is simply the fact that *a* is *F*.

[5] Sextus Empiricus, *Outlines of Pyrrhonism*, Book I, Chap. 6, in Vol. I of *Sextus Empiricus*, The Loeb Classical Library (Cambridge: Harvard University Press, 1933).

Whenever this type of answer is appropriate, we have encountered what is directly evident.

An attempt   At first consideration, one might suppose that those statements
to escape   that correctly describe our "experience," or formulate our "perceptions" or "observations," are statements expressing what is directly evident in the sense described. But what is expressed by such statements does not satisfy the criteria we have just set forth.

In answer to the question "What is my justification for thinking I know that Mr. Smith is here?" one may say, "I see that he is here." But "I see that he is here" does not express what is directly evident in our present sense of the term. For in reply to the question "What is my justification for counting it as evident that it is Mr. *Smith* that I see?" a reasonable man will *not* say, "What justifies me in counting it as evident that I see Mr. Smith is simply the fact that I do see Mr. Smith." If he understands the Socratic question, he will say instead something like: "I know that Mr. Smith is a tall man with red hair; I see a tall man with red hair; I know that no one else satisfying that description would be in this room now. . . ." Each of these propositions in turn, including "I see a tall man with red hair," would be justified by reference to still other propositions. And this is true of any other perceptual proposition. Hence, we cannot say that what we know by means of perception or observation is itself something that is directly evident.

There are philosophers who might say, "What justifies me in counting it as evident that Mr. Smith is here (or that I see Mr. Smith) is simply my present *experience*; but the experience itself cannot be said to be evident, much less to have evidence conferred upon it." With this reply they may suppose themselves able to circumvent some of the more difficult questions of the theory of knowledge.[6] Yet the reply seems clearly to make room for further Socratic questioning. For we may ask, "What justifies me in counting it as evident that my experience is of such a sort that experiences of that sort make it evident to me that Mr. Smith is here, or that I see that Mr. Smith is here?" And to this question one could reasonably reply in the way described above.

States that   The following quotation from Leibniz points to what is directly
present   evident:
themselves

> Our direct awareness of our own existence and of our own thoughts provides us with the primary truths *a posteriori*, the primary truths of fact, or, in other words, our primary experiences; just as identical propositions constitute the primary truths *a priori*, the primary truths

---

[6] See Leonard Nelson's *Über das sogenannte Erkenntnisproblem* (Göttingen: Verlag "Öffentliches Leben," 1930), reprinted from *Abhandlungen der Fries'schen Schule*, II (Göttingen: Verlag "Öffentliches Leben," 1908), especially 479-85, 502-3, 521-24, 528. Cf. "The Impossibility of the 'Theory of Knowledge,'" in his *Socratic Method and Critical Philosophy*, especially pp. 190-92.

of reason, or, in other words, our primary insights. Neither the one nor the other is capable of being demonstrated and both can be called *immediate*—the former, because there is no mediation between the understanding and its objects, and the latter because there is no mediation between the subject and the predicate.[7]

We are here concerned with Leibniz's "primary truths of fact." The "primary truths of reason" will be discussed in Chapter 5.

Thinking and believing provide us with paradigm cases of the directly evident. Consider a reasonable man who is thinking about Albuquerque, or who believes that Albuquerque is in New Mexico, and suppose him to reflect on the philosophical question "What is my justification for counting it as evident, or for thinking that I know, that I am thinking about Albuquerque, or that I believe that Albuquerque is in New Mexico?" (He is *not* asking "What is my justification for thinking that Albuquerque is in New Mexico?") He could reply in the following way: "My justification for counting it as evident that I am thinking about Albuquerque, or that I believe that Albuquerque is in New Mexico, is simply the fact that I *am* thinking about Albuquerque, or that I *do* believe that it is in New Mexico." And this reply fits our formula for the directly evident:

> What justifies me in counting it as evident that *a* is *F* is simply the fact that *a* is *F*.

The man has justified a proposition merely by reiterating it, and this type of justification is *not* appropriate in connection with the questions that were previously discussed. To the question "What justification do you have for counting it as evident that there can be no life on the moon?" it would be inappropriate—and impertinent—simply to reiterate "There can be no life on the moon." But we can state our justification for certain propositions about our *beliefs*, and certain propositions about our thoughts, merely by reiterating those propositions. They may be said, therefore, to pertain to what is directly evident.

Borrowing a technical term from Meinong, let us say that what is directly evident to a man is always some state of affairs that "presents itself to him." Thus, my believing that Socrates is mortal is a state of affairs that is "self-presenting" to me. If I do believe that Socrates is mortal, then, *ipso facto*, it is evident to me that I believe that Socrates is mortal; the state of affairs is "apprehended through itself." [8]

---

[7] *New Essays Concerning Human Understanding*, Book IV, Chap. 9.

[8] See A. Meinong, *Über emotionale Präsentation* (Vienna: Alfred Hölder, 1917), Sec. 1. Cf. Franz Brentano, *Psychologie vom empirischen Standpunkt* (Leipzig: Felix Meiner, 1924), Chap. 2, Sec. 2; Bertrand Russell, *An Inquiry into Meaning and Truth* (New York: W. W. Norton & Company, Inc., 1940), chaps. 9-11; Ledger Wood, *The Analysis of Knowledge* (Princeton: Princeton University Press, 1941), Chap. 5; and C. J. Ducasse, "Propositions, Truth, and the Ultimate Criterion of Truth," *Philosophy and Phenomenological Research*, IV (1944), 317-40.

Other states that may be similarly self-presenting are those described by "thinking that one remembers that . . ." or "seeming to remember that . . ." (as distinguished from "remembering that . . ."), and "taking" or "thinking that one perceives" (as distinguished from "perceiving"). Desiring, hoping, wondering, wishing, loving, hating may also be self-presenting. These states are what Leibniz intended by the term "thoughts." But the area of what is self-presenting may be somewhat wider than that of our thoughts, if we take the latter term in its ordinary sense.

It has been suggested, for example, that our own actions can be known "without observation"—that a man can know directly and immediately what it is that he is doing at any particular time without observing his actions by means of any of the senses.[9] However, it might be more accurate to say that a man can know directly and "without observation" what it is that he means or intends to be doing—what it is that he is trying or undertaking to do. For where his action is an overt, bodily action, he cannot know "without observation" what it is that he is succeeding in doing; he cannot know, without observation, what the actual effects of his trying or undertaking happen to be. The fact remains, however, that trying or undertaking is more than merely thinking and that trying or undertaking is also "self-presenting." We may say, therefore, that Leibniz was mistaken in restricting the "primary truths of fact" to "our direct awareness of our own existence and of our own thoughts." Statements about what a man is trying or undertaking to do at any particular time are not, strictly speaking, statements about his "thoughts," but they are statements which do express what is directly evident to him at that time.

An alternative description But surely, one may object, it makes no sense whatever to ask "What is your justification for thinking you know that you believe that Socrates is mortal?"

To one who feels that such questions "make no sense," we need not reply by trying to show him that they do. It is enough to make two points: (1) If he is right, then such propositions as "I believe that Socrates is mortal" and "I am thinking about the moon" differ in one very important respect from such propositions as "Socrates is mortal" and "There can be no life on the moon." The former propositions, if our critic is right, are such that it "makes no sense" to ask, with respect to them, "What is my justification for thinking I know that they are true?" (2) Yet they resemble propositions which *are* known to be true in that they may function as *evidence*. My evidence that you and I think alike with respect to the mortality of Socrates cannot consist solely of the evidence I have concerning *your* beliefs about Socrates. It must also

[9] Cf. G. E. M. Anscombe, *Intention* (Oxford: Basil Blackwell, 1957), pp. 49-50.

consist of the fact that *I* believe that Socrates is mortal. And these two points provide us with an alternative way of characterizing the directly evident.

We could say paradoxically that a proposition is *directly evident* to a man provided (1) that it makes no sense to say of him that he knows the proposition to be true, and (2) that the proposition is evidence for him of something else.

If we use our original characterization of the directly evident, we might think of the directly evident as that which "constitutes its own evidence," and therefore, in the terms of Sextus Empiricus, as that which is "apprehended through itself." But if we use the alternative characterization, we may think paradoxically of the directly evident as being that which is "evidence but not evident." [10] In the one case, we are reminded of the prime mover that moves itself, and in the other, of the prime mover unmoved.

It will be convenient to continue with the terms of our original characterization, but what we shall say can readily be translated into those of the second.

We have yet to consider the most interesting—and controversial—examples of the directly evident.

Seeming and   In the second of his *Méditations*, Descartes offers what he takes to
appearing   be good reasons for doubting whether, on any occasion, he sees
light, hears noise, or feels heat, and he then observes: "Let it be so; still it is at least quite *certain that it seems to me that* I see light, that I hear noise and that I feel heat." [11] This observation about seeming should be contrasted with what St. Augustine says, in his *Contra Academicos*, about appearing.

> I do not see how the Academician can refute him who says: "I know that this appears white to me, I know that my hearing is delighted with this, I know that this has an agreeable odor, I know that this tastes sweet to me, I know that this feels cold to me." . . . I say this that, when a person tastes something, he can honestly swear that he

---

[10] The second method of characterization is in the spirit of the following observations by Ludwig Wittgenstein: (1) "It can't be said of me at all (except perhaps as a joke) that I *know* I'm in pain" and (2) "Justification by experience comes to an end. If it did not it would not be justification." *Philosophical Investigations* (Oxford: Basil Blackwell, 1953), pp. 89e, 136e. From the fact that it can't be said of me that I know that I'm in pain, it will not follow, of course, that it *can* be said of me that I do not know—i.e., that I am ignorant of the fact—that I am in pain.

[11] E. S. Haldane and R. T. Ross, eds., *The Philosophical Works of Descartes*, I (London: Cambridge University Press, 1934), 153; my italics. The French reads: ". . . *il est certain qu'il me semble que je vois de la lumière, que j'entends du bruit et que je sens de la chaleur.*"

knows it is sweet to his palate or the contrary, and that no trickery of the Greeks can dispossess him of that knowledge.[12]

These two passages remind us that such words as "seem" or "appear" have different uses in different contexts.

Thus, Descartes' expression, "It seems to me that I see light," when uttered on any ordinary occasion, might be taken to be performing one or the other of two quite different functions. (1) The expression might be used simply to report one's belief; in such a case, "It seems to me that I see light" could be replaced by "I believe that I see light." Taken in this way, the "seems"-statement expresses what is directly evident, but since it is equivalent to a belief-statement it does not add anything to the cases we have already considered. (2) "It seems to me"—or better, "It seems to *me*"—may be used not only to report a belief, but also to provide the speaker with a way out, a kind of hedge, in case the statement prefixed by "It seems to me" should turn out to be false. This function of "It seems" is thus the contrary of the performative function of "I know" to which J. L. Austin has called attention. In saying "I know," I give my hearers a kind of guarantee and, as Austin says, stake my reputation; but in saying "It seems to *me*," I play it safe, indicating to them that what I say carries no guarantee at all and that if they choose to believe what I say they do so entirely at their own risk.[13] "It seems to me," used in this way, cannot be said to describe what is directly evident, for it cannot be said to describe anything at all.

But the word "appear" as it is used in the translation from St. Augustine—"This appears white to me"—performs still another function. (3) It may be used to describe a certain state of affairs which is not itself a belief. When "appear" is used in this descriptive, "phenomenological" way, one may say consistently and without any incongruity, "That thing appears white to me in this light, but I know that it is really grey." One may also say, again, consistently and without any incongruity, "It appears white to me in this light and I know that, as a matter of fact, it *is* white."

The latter statement illustrates two points overlooked by many contemporary philosophers, the first being that in such a statement, "appear" cannot have the hedging use just referred to, for if it did, the statement would be incongruous (which it is not). The second part ("I know that it is white") would provide a guarantee which the first part ("This appears white") withholds. The second point is that the

[12] *Against the Academicians (Contra Academicos)*, trans. and ed. Sister Mary Patricia Garvey (Milwaukee: Marquette University Press, 1942), para. 26, p. 68 of translation.
[13] Austin discussed this use of "seems" in considerable detail in his posthumous *Sense and Sensibilia* (Oxford: The Clarendon Press, 1962).

descriptive, phenomenological use of "appears" is not restricted to the description of *illusory* experiences.

The following translation from Sextus Empiricus reminds us that "seems," as well as a number of other verbs, has this descriptive, phenomenological use:

> The same water which feels very hot when poured on inflamed spots seems lukewarm to us. And the same air seems chilly to the old but mild to those in their prime, and similarly the same sound seems to the former faint, but to the latter clearly audible. The same wine which seems sour to those who have previously eaten dates or figs seems sweet to those who have just consumed nuts or chickpeas; and the vestibule of the bathhouse which warms those entering from the outside chills those coming out.[14]

Sextus is here using certain appear-words to indicate a fact about our experience that is familiar to us all—namely, the fact that by varying the state of the subject or perceiver, or of the intervening medium, or of other conditions of observation, we may also vary the ways in which the objects that the subject perceives will appear to him. Sextus' appear-statements are simply descriptive of experience.

Some of these descriptive "appear"- and "seem"-statements may describe what is self-presenting, and when they do, what they express is directly evident. We can single out such a class of directly evident "appear"-statements by referring to what Aristotle called the "proper objects" of the various senses and to what he called the "common sensibles." [15] The "proper objects" may be illustrated by the following: visual characteristics such as blue, green, yellow, red, white, black; auditory characteristics such as sounding or making a noise; somesthetic characteristics such as rough, smooth, hard, soft, heavy, light, hot, cold; gustatory characteristics such as sweet, sour, salt, bitter; and olfactory characteristics, such as fragrant, spicy, putrid, burned. The "common sensibles" are those characteristics such as movement, rest, number, figure, and magnitude, which, as Aristotle says, "are not peculiar to any one sense, but are common to all."

If for any such characteristic *F*, I can justify a claim to knowledge by saying of something that it *appears F* (by saying of the wine that it now *looks* red, or *tastes* sour, to me), where the verb is intended in the descriptive, phenomenological sense just indicated, then the *appearing* in question is self-presenting and my statement expresses what is directly evident. The claim that I thus justify, by saying of something that it appears *F*, may be the claim that the thing *is F*, but as we have seen, it

---

[14] *Outlines of Pyrrhonism*, Book I, Chap. 14; abridged from Vol. I of *Sextus Empiricus*, The Loeb Classical Library, pp. 55, 63, 65. Cf. K. Lykos, "Aristotle and Plato on 'Appearing,'" *Mind*, LXXIII (1964), 496-514.

[15] See Aristotle's *De Anima*, Book II, chaps. 6 and 7.

may also be some other claim. To the question "What justification do I have for thinking I know, or for counting it as evident, that something now *looks* red to me, or *tastes* sour?" I could reply only by reiterating that something does now look red or taste sour.[16]

Strictly speaking, "The *wine* tastes sour to me" and "*Something* looks red to me" do not express what is directly evident in our sense of this term. For the first statement implies that I am tasting *wine* and the second that there is a certain thing that is appearing red to me, and "I am tasting wine" and "There is a certain physical thing that is appearing red to me" do not express what is directly evident. What justifies me in counting it as evident that I am tasting wine is *not* simply the fact that I am tasting wine, and what justifies me in counting it as evident that a certain physical thing is appearing red to me (and that I am not, say, merely suffering from an hallucination) is not simply the fact that a certain thing *is* appearing red to me. To arrive at what is directly evident in these cases, we must remove the reference to wine in "The wine tastes sour to me" and we must remove the reference to the appearing thing in "That thing appears red to me." This, however, is very difficult to do, since our language was not developed for any such philosophical purpose.

Many philosophers and psychologists would turn verbs into substantives, saying in the one case, "I have a sour taste," and in the other, "I am experiencing a red appearance." Such a procedure has the advantage of enabling us to assimilate these seemings and appearings to other types of sensuous experience—to feelings, imagery, and the sensuous content of dreams and hallucinations, all of which may be "self-presenting" in the sense we have described. But in introducing the substantive "appearance," we may seem to be multiplying entities beyond necessity; for now we seem to be saying that *appearances*, as well as fences and houses, may be counted among the entities that are red. "I have a sour taste" may suggest, similarly, that *tastes*, like wine and fruit, are among the entities that may be sour. It is clear that we must proceed with great care if we are to employ this substantival terminology.[17]

[16] Or if the directly evident is to be viewed in analogy with the prime mover unmoved instead of with the prime mover that moves itself, I could say (1) that it "makes no sense" to say "It is evident to me that something now looks red or tastes sour" and (2) that "Something now looks red" or "Something now tastes sour" may yet formulate my *evidence* for something else.

[17] One of the first philosophers to note the pitfalls which this substantival, or "sense datum," terminology involves was Thomas Reid; see his *Inquiry into the Human Mind* (1764), Chap. 6, Sec. 20, and *Essays on the Intellectual Powers* (1785), Essay II, Chap. 16. Cf. H. A. Prichard, *Kant's Theory of Knowledge* (Oxford: The Clarendon Press, 1909), and "Appearances and Reality," *Mind* (1906); the latter is reprinted in *Realism and the Background of Phenomenology*, ed. Roderick M. Chisholm (New York: Free Press of Glencoe, Inc., 1960). We shall return to "the metaphysical status of appearances" in Chap. 6.

Let us consider another way of describing these self-presenting states. In our examples, "appear" requires a grammatical subject and thus requires a term that purports to refer not merely to a way of appearing, but also to a thing that is said to appear in that way. However, we may eliminate the reference to the thing that appears if we convert our appear-sentences: Instead of saying "Something appears white to me," we may say, more awkwardly, "I am appeared white to by something." We may then eliminate the substantival "something" by merely dropping the final clause, saying, "I am appeared white to." [18] The verbs "tastes" and "sounds" do not allow a similar conversion of "This tastes sour" and "That sounds loud," but "is appeared to" could replace such verbs: We could say "I am appeared loud to" and "I am appeared sour to," just as we have said "I am appeared white to." The words "loud," "sour," and "white," in these sentences, do not function as adjectives; the sentences do not say, of any entity, that that entity *is* loud, sour, or white. The words are used here to describe *ways* of appearing, or of being appeared to, just as "swift" and "slow" may be used to describe ways of running. They function as adverbs and our sentences would be more correct, therefore, if they were put as: "I am appeared sourly to," "I am appeared whitely to," and "I am appeared loudly to."

The awkwardness of the "appears to" terminology could be avoided if, at this point, we were to introduce another verb, say, "sense," using it in a technical way as a synonym for "is appeared to." In this case, we would say "I sense sourly," "I sense whitely," and "I sense loudly." But even this procedure will introduce ambiguities, as the third example suggests.

Once these terminological difficulties have been removed, is there ground for doubt concerning the directly evident character of what is expressed by statements about appearing? Doubts have been raised in recent years and we should consider these briefly.

Some mis-
conceptions
There are *some* descriptive appear-statements that do not express what is directly evident—for example, "He looks just the way his uncle did fifteen years ago." If we describe a way of appearing by *comparing* it with the way in which some physical thing happens to have appeared in the past, or with the way in which some physical thing is thought normally to appear, then the justification for what we say about the way of appearing will depend in part upon the justification for what we say about the physical thing; and what we say about the physical thing will not now be directly evident. It has been argued that the types of ap-

---

[18] But the substantival "I" remains. Recall the beginning of our quotation from Leibniz: "Our direct awareness of our own existence and of our thoughts provides us with the primary truths *a posteriori* . . ." (see p. 27).

pear-statements we have just been considering *also* involve some comparison with previously experienced objects, and hence, that what they express cannot ever be said to be directly evident. It has been suggested that if I say "This appears white," I am making a "comparison between a present object and a formerly seen object." [19] What justification is there for saying this?

"Appears white" *may* be used to abbreviate "appears the way in which white things normally appear." But "white thing," on the other hand, *may* be used to abbreviate "thing having the color of things that normally appear white." The phrase "appear white," as it is used in the latter expression, is *not* used to abbreviate "appear the way in which white things normally appear," for the point of the previous sentence cannot be expressed by saying that "white thing" may be used to abbreviate "thing having the color of things which ordinarily appear the way in which *white things* normally appear." Therefore, when we say that "white thing" may be used to abbreviate "thing having the color of things that ordinarily appear white," the point of "appear white" is not to compare a way of appearing with anything. In this use of "appears white," we may say significantly and without redundancy, "Things that *are* white normally *appear* white." And this is the way in which we should interpret "This appears white to me" in the quotation above (see p. 30) from St. Augustine. More generally, it is in terms of this descriptive, noncomparative use of our other "appear"- and "seem"-words (including "looks," "tastes," "sounds," and the like) that we are to interpret those appear-statements that are said to be directly evident.

But philosophers have offered three different arguments to show that appear-words cannot be used in this noncomparative way. Each of the three arguments, I believe, is quite obviously inconclusive.

(1) To attempt to derive a conclusion about the meaning of "appear" and similar words, the first argument makes use of a certain hypothesis which states how people acquire their language. The hypothesis states that sentences such as "This appears white" are "parasitical upon" sentences such as "This *is* white"; that is to say, in order to understand "This appears white," one must *first* be able to understand "This is white." It is then inferred that there is an important sense of the expression "really means" which is such that (a) "This appears white" *can* be said, in that sense, really to mean the same as "This appears in the way in which white things ordinarily appear," and which is such that (b) "This is white" *cannot* be said really to mean the same as "This is the sort of thing that ordinarily appears white," where "appears white" is used in the way we have just described. If this argument were

---

[19] Hans Reichenbach, *Experience and Prediction* (Chicago: University of Chicago Press, 1938), p. 176.

valid, then there would be no clear sense in which what is expressed by "This appears white" could be said to be directly evident; to state our justification for thinking that we know that a certain thing appears white, we would need to state our justification for our belief about the ways in which white things normally appear. But the argument is invalid. Even if the linguistic hypothesis upon which the argument is based were true, the conclusion does not follow. From premises telling us that in order to learn the meaning of a certain expression *A*, one must first learn the meaning of a certain expression *B*, we cannot derive the conclusion that *A* really means the same as *B*.

(2) It has also been argued: "If the sentence 'I am appeared white to' does not express a comparison between a present way of appearing and anything else, then the sentence is completely empty and says nothing at all about a present way of appearing. But if it expresses what is directly evident, then it cannot assert a comparison between a present way of appearing and anything else. Therefore, either 'I am appeared white to' is empty or it does not express what is directly evident." Here the difficulty lies in the first premise. It may be true that if an appear-sentence is to communicate anything, it must assert some comparison of things; if I wish you to know the way in which I am appeared to now, I must relate this way of being appeared to with something that is familiar to you. ("Describe the taste? It's something like the taste of a mango.") But our question is not: "If you are to understand me when I say something about the way in which I am appeared to, must I be comparing that way of appearing with the way in which some object, familiar to you, happens to appear?" The question is, more simply: "Can I apprehend the way in which I am now appeared to without thereby supposing, with respect to some object, that the way I am being appeared to is the way in which that object sometimes appears or has sometimes appeared?" From the fact that the first of these two questions must be answered in the negative, it does not follow that the second must also be answered in the negative.[20]

(3) The final argument designed to show that appear-statements cannot express what is directly evident, may be put as follows: "(a) In saying 'Something appears white,' you are making certain assumptions

---

[20] Actually, the argument in question seems to presuppose a more general thesis about the nature of thought or predication, a thesis that might be expressed by saying that "all judgments are comparative." But to see that this thesis is absurd, we have only to formulate it precisely. The thesis tells us that in order to assert or to believe, with respect to any particular thing *x*, that *x* has a certain property *F*, one must *compare* *x* with some other thing *y* and thus assert or believe of *x* that it has something in common with that other thing *y*. But clearly, we cannot derive "*x* is *F*" from "*x* resembles *y*" unless, among other things, we can say or believe *noncomparatively* that *y* is *F*.

about language; you are assuming, for example, that the word 'white,' or the phrase 'appears white,' is being used in the way in which you have used it on other occasions, or in the way in which other people have used it. Therefore (b), when you say 'This appears white,' you are saying something not only about your present experience, but also about all of these other occasions. But (c) what you are saying about these other occasions is not directly evident. And therefore (d), 'This is white' does not express what is directly evident."

The false step in this argument is the inference from (a) to (b). We must distinguish the belief that a speaker has about the words that he is using from the belief that he is using those words to express. What holds true for the former need not hold true for the latter. A Frenchman, believing that "potatoes" is English for apples, may use "There are potatoes in the basket" to express the belief that there are apples in the basket; from the fact that he has a mistaken belief about "potatoes" and "apples," it does not follow that he has a mistaken belief about potatoes and apples. Similarly, it may be that what a man believes about his own use of the expression "appears white" is something that is not directly evident to him—indeed what he believes about his own language may even be false and unreasonable; but from these facts it does not follow that what he intends to assert when he utters "This appears white to me" is something that cannot be directly evident.

We have, then, singled out various types of statements expressing what is directly evident. Most of these statements, as Leibniz said, refer to our *thoughts*; they may say what we are thinking, believing, hoping, fearing, wishing, wondering, desiring, loving, hating; or they may say what we think we know, or think we are remembering, or think we are perceiving. Some of them will refer to our *actions*, at least to the extent of saying what we are trying or undertaking to do at any particular time. And some of them will refer to ways in which we *sense*, or are *appeared* to.

But clearly, what we *know* is not restricted to what is directly evident.

THE INDIRECTLY EVIDENT

3

The relation
of the directly
evident to
the indirectly
evident Those "truths of fact" that are known but are not directly evident may be said to be indirectly evident. Hence, whatever we know about "external objects," other people, and the past, may be said to be indirectly evident. Traditionally, the theory of knowledge, or that part of it that we might call the "theory of evidence," has proceeded from the assumption that the indirectly evident is "based upon" or "known through" the directly evident. This assumption may be taken to imply that there are certain epistemic principles or rules of evidence which, in application to what is directly evident, will yield whatever is indirectly evident. By means of these principles, it is assumed, what we know about "external objects," other people, and the past may somehow be derived from those truths about our thoughts, undertakings, and ways of being appeared to that constitute the directly evident. While we shall proceed here upon this traditional assumption, in the following chapter we shall consider the assumption itself and discuss some of the methodological problems to which it gives rise.

By means of what principles, then, could the indirectly evident be derived from the directly evident?

Not a
deductive
relation The principles of evidence that we now seek may well include the ordinary principles of deductive logic. But application of such deductive principles to the directly evident will not of itself be sufficient to yield any of the things that we are now assuming to be indirectly evident. For the directly evident premises that are available to us at any given moment, could be expressed in statements of the following sort.

38

I take something to be a cat on the roof.
I seem to recall that it was here before.
I am thinking about a horse.
I am trying to get across the street.
I am appeared greenly to.

The only significant deductive consequences that can be drawn from such directly evident premises will be other statements about the self, or about thoughts, undertakings, and appearances. But the indirectly evident conclusions that we wish to derive can be expressed in statements such as:

There is a cat on the roof.
It was also here yesterday.
Part of it is green.

Hence, any principles that enable us to derive the indirectly evident from the directly evident will not be the principles of deduction.

Nor will they be the principles of induction.

Not an inductive relation Let us consider the nature of induction and ask ourselves what types of inductive argument *would* support the conclusion "There is a cat on the roof." Broadly speaking, we may say there are two.

In the one case, the premises of the argument are "factual," synthetic statements enumerating certain facts about cats and roofs or about certain things bearing a significant resemblance to cats and roofs.

There is a cat on the roof of the first house.
There is a cat on the roof of the second house.
There is a cat on the roof of the third house.
This is the fourth house.
▶ Therefore, in all probability, there is a cat on the roof of this house.

Again:

There was a cat on the roof yesterday.
There was a cat on the roof the day before yesterday.
There was a cat on the roof the day before that.
▶ Therefore, in all probability, there is a cat on the roof today.

Or, again:

There is a sheep in front of that house, a horse in the back, a dog inside, and a cat on the roof.
There is a sheep in front of this house, a horse in the back, and a dog inside.
▶ Therefore, in all probability, there is a cat on the roof of this house.

Clearly, we have no directly evident premises to enable us to construct any such enumerative inductive argument for supporting the conclusion that a cat is on the roof. For as we have seen, every directly evident statement pertains to the thoughts or undertakings of the self or to the ways in which one is appeared to.

Induction may be construed somewhat more broadly, however. Any argument of the following sort could also be said to be an inductive argument for a given hypothesis: The premises tell us, first, some of the things that would be true *if* the hypothesis were true, and secondly, that some of these things *are* true (possibly they will record the outcome of a favorable test or experiment). Thus, we might appeal to a generalization telling us some of the things that would happen if a cat were on the roof. We then perform a test or experiment to see whether these things are happening; if we find that they are, we argue that our hypothesis has been confirmed.

> If there is a cat on the roof and if I stand in the garden and look toward the roof, then I will see something that I will take to be a cat.
> I am standing in the garden and looking toward the roof.
> I see something I take to be a cat.
> ▶ Therefore, in all probability, a cat is on the roof.

Other instances of this type of inductive argument may be considerably more complex, but in every case the premises will include a synthetic, "factual" statement, corresponding to the first statement above, telling us some of the things that would follow if the conclusion happened to be true.

It is now clear that we cannot argue in this way, from directly evident premises to "A cat is on the roof." For our premises will include no "factual," synthetic statement telling us what would happen if a cat were on the roof.[1]

What we have said can readily be seen to hold true for any of those other things that we have described as being indirectly evident. It would seem reasonable to conclude, therefore, that if the indirectly evident can be derived from the directly evident, then there are principles of derivation which are neither deductive nor inductive. What, then, could these principles be?

---

[1] There are certain logical or "nonfactual" truths that might be thought to tell us what would happen if a cat were on the roof (for example, "If a cat is on the roof, then an animal is on the roof"). But the addition of any such logical truth to our premises would not help matters. For whatever conclusion can be demonstrated deductively or inductively, by means of a set of premises that includes a logical truth, can also be demonstrated by means of the set that remains if we omit that logical truth. The concept of *logical truth* will be discussed in Chap. 4.

The theory of Carneades

If there is a solution to our problem, it is likely to be a version of the theory of Carneades of Cyrene (c. 213–129 B.C.), one of the leaders of the Platonic Academy and the most important of the "Academic Sceptics." Carneades' theory, as it is set forth by Sextus Empiricus in his *Outlines of Pyrrhonism* and in his treatise *Against the Logicians,* involves three theses concerning the "evidence of the senses."

In discussing Carneades' theses, we will make use of three of the epistemic terms introduced in Chapter 1. We suggested there that a proposition can be called "acceptable" (for a given person at a given time) if withholding it is not more reasonable than believing it; it can be called "reasonable" if believing it is more reasonable than withholding it; and it can be called "evident" if it is reasonable and if there is no proposition more reasonable than it. Thus, whatever is evident is reasonable, but not conversely, and whatever is reasonable is acceptable, but not conversely.

(1) We may put Carneades' first thesis by saying: If a man has a perception of something having a certain property *F*, then, for him, the proposition that there *is* something having that property *F* is acceptable. If he has a perception of something being a cat, for example, then, for him, the proposition that there is a cat is acceptable.[2]

But why must we use awkward terminology? Instead of "He has a perception of something being a cat," why not simply say, "He perceives something to be a cat"? And why not use "evident" instead of merely "acceptable"? If a man *perceives* something to be a cat, then, after all, he *knows* that there is a cat; the proposition is evident and not merely acceptable.

Carneades might well reply: To be sure, if a man perceives something to be *F*, then the proposition that there is an *F* is evident to him. But if our principle is expressed in this way, it can no longer be applied. For the man has no way of deciding, on any particular occasion, that he *does* perceive anything to be *F*. His experience, on any particular occasion, provides him with no guarantee that he *is* perceiving a cat.

Consider a case in which, as we sometimes put it, a man's senses have "deceived him." He takes something to be a cat and he can say honestly and sincerely that he "sees a cat"; yet what he sees is not a cat at all. His experience, at the time at which he has it, is one that he cannot distinguish from that experience which *is* correctly called "perceiving a cat"—from that experience which, if it were to occur, would make evident the proposition that the thing in question is a cat. If we

---

[2] Carneades' own term is generally translated as "probable," not as "acceptable." But in view of the contemporary use of "probable" and the use that we have assigned to "acceptable," the latter is preferred in the present context.

use "perceive" in its ordinary way, we cannot say that, at the time of the deceptive experience, the man "perceived a cat." We must describe the experience in some other way—hence, the awkward "He has a perception of something being a cat."

If there were a way of distinguishing "veridical" perceptions, when we have them, from those that are "unveridical," we could formulate our principle by reference solely to the former. But the senses, "one and all," can "play us false"; hence, the most we can say, on any particular occasion, is that we are "having a perception"—a perception which may or may not be veridical.[3] We can say, for Carneades (he did not say it himself), that it may be directly evident to a man, on a particular occasion, that he is "having a perception of a cat," but it is never directly evident to a man that he is "perceiving a cat." Hence, if our epistemic principles are to be applied to what is "directly evident," we must refer to "having a perception of something being *F*," and not to "perceiving an *F*."

(2) Having delineated a class of propositions that are acceptable, Carneades now proceeds to single out a certain subclass of these propositions. Some of our perceptions, he tells us, concur and re-enforce each other, "hanging together like links in a chain."[4] These perceptions he describes as being "uncontradicted and concurring"; each of them attests to the same fact and none of them casts doubt upon any of the others. In illustrating Carneades' view, Sextus cites a group of perceptions all concurring in the fact that a certain man is Socrates. "We believe that this man is Socrates from the fact that he possesses all his customary qualities—colour, size, shape, converse, coat, and his position in a place where there is no one like him." Concurrence is also illustrated in medical diagnoses: "Some doctors do not deduce that it is a true case of fever from one symptom only—such as too quick a pulse or a very high temperature—but from a concurrence, such as that of a high temperature with a rapid pulse and ulcerous joints and flushing and thirst and analogous symptoms."[5] Carneades' second thesis, then, is this: Acceptable propositions that stand in this relation of concurrence are more reasonable than those that do not.

As the examples suggest, Carneades must appeal to independent information—or at least to some independent set of beliefs—in order to determine whether the members of a set of perceptions happen to "concur." The perception of Socrates' coat concurs with that of his size and

---

[3] Sextus Empiricus, *Against the Logicians*, Book I, para. 160, in Vol. II of *Sextus Empiricus*, The Loeb Classical Library (Cambridge: Harvard University Press, 1933), p. 87.
[4] *Ibid.*, para. 176, p. 95.
[5] *Ibid.*, para. 178-79, p. 97.

shape only in virtue of the fact, memory, or belief that Socrates *has* such and such a coat and such and such a size and shape. It is a defect of Carneades' account, therefore, or at least of the account that has been reported to us, that he provides no way of deciding *what* independent beliefs may be used in thus establishing concurrence. And he does not tell us exactly what concurrence is; I shall attempt to describe it in more detail below.

(3) Finally, from the class of "uncontradicted and concurring" perceptions just described, Carneades singles out a further subset—those perceptions having the additional virtue of being "closely scrutinized and tested." In "testing" a perception, we "scrutinize" the conditions under which it occurred. We examine the conditions of observation—the intervening medium, our sense organs, and our own state of mind. The perception survives these tests if we find the following:

> that we have our senses in good order, and that we see the object when wide awake and not asleep, and that there exists at the same time a clear atmosphere and a moderate distance and immobility on the part of the object perceived, so that because of these conditions the presentation is trustworthy, we having had sufficient time for the scrutiny of the facts observed at the seat of the presentation.[6]

In thus scrutinizing any particular perception, we appeal to other perceptions (e.g., our perception of the state of the atmosphere) and we also appeal to independent information or beliefs (e.g., the information or beliefs we must utilize in deciding whether the senses are "in good order"). Once again, Carneades fails to tell us *what* independent information and beliefs we are entitled to appeal to.[7]

Carneades' third thesis, then, is this: Concurrent propositions that survive such "close scrutiny and test" are more reasonable than those that do not. Apparently, however, he would not go so far as to say that they are "reasonable" in the sense of the term that we have defined; for he is not quoted as saying categorically that accepting these propositions is more reasonable than withholding them. And he denies that they are propositions that we know to be true, for, he says, they are not

---

[6] *Ibid.*, para. 188, p. 103.

[7] It is interesting to note that Carneades seems to have an up-to-date view about the relation between appearances, or the ways in which we are appeared to, and what we know. He suggests, first, that "scrutiny" of appearances does not normally occur unless some belief is being tested. As Thomas Reid and others were later to say, the mind normally "passes through" the appearances and focuses directly upon the things that appear. Carneades insists, secondly, that nothing is evident to us, and therefore, is committed to the view that our apprehension of the ways in which we are appeared to is not directly evident. Indeed, St. Augustine's remarks about appearances, quoted in the preceding chapter, were written in criticism of Carneades' views. But it may be that Carneades accepted what I have called "the prime mover unmoved" view of our apprehension of the ways in which we are appeared to.

evident. His justification for saying they are not evident is the fact that the criteria he sets forth provide us with no guarantee of *truth*: A proposition may pass these tests and yet be false.[8] Carneades has given us, therefore, a version of scepticism.

It may be, however, that by following Carneades' general procedure, we will find what we are looking for—a way in which the indirectly evident can be said to be "known through" or "based upon" the directly evident.

The remainder of this chapter may be thought of as a preliminary sketch or outline of one possible theory of empirical evidence. We shall set forth nine epistemic principles.

"Self-presentation" and perception   We may suppose, once again, that we are dealing with a rational person, Mr. *S*, who is conducting a "critique of cogency" of the kind we tried to describe in the preceding chapter. Mr. *S* asks himself, with respect to various things that he knows or thinks he knows, what his justification is for thinking that he knows those things. And, it will be recalled, he asks himself these questions not to discredit or cast doubt upon his knowledge, but in order to elicit certain general principles about the nature of knowledge and of evidence.

In answer to the question "What is my justification for thinking that I know such and such?" Mr. *S* may say: "My justification for thinking that I know such and such is the fact that I know so and so, and if I know so and so, then I know such and such." Let us express this briefly by saying: *S* justifies his claim or belief that he knows such and such by appeal to the proposition that he knows so and so.

Unlike Carneades, we will countenance the directly evident character of *S*'s "self-presenting states." The first of our nine epistemic principles may be summarized as follows:

(A)   If there is a "self-presenting state" such that *S* is in that state, then it is *evident* to *S* that he is in that state.

And now, like Carneades, we may turn to perception. But we will single out two subspecies of perception and say, of the one, that it presents us with what is *reasonable,* and of the other, that it presents us with what is *evident.*

Let us suppose that *S* knows, or thinks he knows, with respect to a certain property or relation *F*, that there is something that has that property *F* or stands in that relation *F*. Taking the word "justify" in the

---

[8] Cicero expresses this point by saying that "the perceptions of what is true are all of such a kind that a perception of what is false might also be of that same kind"; he adds that this fact seems to constitute the most important argument in favor of scepticism. *Academica*, Book II, Chap. 4, in *Cicero, De Natura Deorum,* The Loeb Classical Library (Cambridge: Harvard University Press, 1933), p. 565.

way we have tried to set forth, let us also suppose that the man would justify his claim to this knowledge, or his belief that he has this knowledge, in the following way: He would appeal to the proposition that he perceives something to be *F* (or sees, hears, feels, or smells something to be *F*, where these latter terms may be taken to imply that he perceives something to be *F*). "My justification for thinking I know that that thing is a sheep is the fact that I *see it to be* a sheep." Let us say that in such a case, *S believes that he perceives* something to be *F*; he believes that he sees something to be a sheep.

"Believing that one perceives" is thus a slightly different concept from Carneades' "having a perception." Consider, for example, what would happen if our Mr. *S* were to see someone in the garden whom he knew to be a thief. It might be natural to say that *S perceives a thief*; and it may be, for all we know, that Carneades would countenance it as being an instance of a *perception of a thief*. But if *S* is honest and rational, like the rest of us, he would not justify "I know him to be a thief" by appeal to "I perceive him to be a thief." That is to say, in answer to the Socratic question "What is my justification for thinking I know that man to be a thief?" *S* would not say that he *perceives him to be* a thief or that he *sees him to be* a thief. And if this is so, then *S* cannot be said, in our sense of the terms, to believe that he perceives a man to be a thief—even though he may be said, in Carneades' sense of the term, to have a perception of a thief.

Our second epistemic principle, then, will be a variant of Carneades' first:

(B)   If *S* believes that he perceives something to have a certain property *F*, then the proposition that he does perceive something to be *F*, as well as the proposition that there is something that is *F*, is one that is *reasonable* for *S*.

For the verb "perceives" in this formula, we may substitute other verbs of the same family—e.g., "sees," "hears," "feels," "observes." And we may understand the expression "to have a property *F*" in such a way that it may be replaced by "to stand, with some thing or things, in a relation *F*."

Principle B is intended to tell us, then, that "believing that one perceives" is a source of reasonable belief. We are, therefore, affirming a version of empiricism.

We may hope that the perceptions which are thus endorsed by our principle form a slightly more respectable group than those with which Carneades began. Carneades does not provide a way of excluding "That man is a thief" from the class of perceptions with which he begins, and it may be, therefore, that he would count "That man is a thief" as being initially acceptable for Mr. S.[9] This would be an undesirable beginning, for the assumption might all too easily survive Carneades' "close scrutiny and test." *S* would have merely to note that he not only sees a thief, but also that he hears one and that he smells one. Our hope, however, is that Principle B will prevent Mr. *S* from beginning in this way. Like Carneades, we are affirming a certain faith in the senses. But we are also affirming a certain faith in the man. We are supposing that Mr. *S* has no belief he would justify by saying "The man is one that I perceive to be a thief." On the basis of this faith, we have assigned a higher evidential status to our perceptions than Carneades assigned to his. We say that, at the very outset, they are reasonable and not merely acceptable; these propositions of perception are such that believing them is more reasonable than withholding them.

The perceptions to which our principle refers are like the perceptions of Carneades in that they may be general and they may be negative (for example, "All the swans in the garden are white" and "There are no other animals there").

They are also like the perceptions of Carneades in that they may be false. Or more exactly, from the fact that *S* believes that he perceives a certain thing to be *F*, it will not follow that there *is* anything that is *F*. Hence, it will not follow either that *S does* perceive something to be *F*. For as we have already noted, if a man does perceive something to be *F*, then (if we take "perceive" in its ordinary sense) he knows that there is something that is *F* and therefore, there *is* something that is *F*.

Perception and the evident

Our third epistemic principle, another thesis concerning perception, will be more bold than anything contained in Carneades' theory of evidence.

Let us return to the "proper objects" of the various senses and to the "common sensibles." The "proper objects," it will be recalled, may be illustrated by reference to the following sensible characteristics: such *visual* characteristics as blue, green, yellow, red, white, black; such *auditory* characteristics as sounding or making a noise; such *somesthetic* characteristics as rough, smooth, hard, soft, heavy, light, hot, cold; such *gustatory* characteristics as sweet, sour, salt, bitter; and such *olfactory* characteristics as fragrant, spicy, putrid, burned. The "common sensibles" are illustrated by such characteristics as movement, rest, number, figure, and magnitude, which, as Aristotle said, "are not peculiar to any sense, but are common to all."

[9] Actually, Carneades restricts his principle to those perceptions that are "vivid and not confused"; conceivably, he took these terms in such a way that they rule out the possibility in question.

For each of the senses there are certain *sensible relations* that are peculiar to the proper objects of that sense. The field of vision provides us with these examples: the relation that holds between any two things, x and y, when x is similar in color to y; the relation that holds among three things, x, y, and z, when x resembles y in color more than it resembles z in color; the relation that holds between any two things, x and y, when x is brighter in color than y; and the relation that holds between any two things, x and y, when x is richer, or more saturated, in color than y. These relations have their analogues in the other sense spheres.

To such relations, we may add other relations pertaining to the "common sensibles": for example, the relation that holds between any two things, x and y, when x is larger than y, or when x moves faster than y, or when x is to the left of y, or when x is above y; the relation that holds among any three things, x, y, and z, when x is nearer to y than to z, or when x is between y and z; and the relation that holds between any two events, x and y, when x temporally precedes y.

Our third principle, then, pertains to those occasions on which S would justify a claim to know by reference to the belief that he perceives something to have some sensible characteristic F. (For brevity, we may count sensible relations as sensible characteristics.) Such occasions, we will say, provide S with propositions that are not only reasonable but are also *evident*:

(C) If there is a certain sensible characteristic F such that S believes that he perceives something to be F, then it is *evident* to S that he is perceiving something to have that characteristic F, and also that there is something that is F.

What we are now saying must be distinguished from our earlier thesis about appearances, or the ways in which a man is appeared to. We said that if S is appeared to red, or blue, or green, or yellow, then it is directly evident to S that he is appeared to in that way. But we are now speaking not merely of the ways in which S is appeared to, but also of things that appear to S. We are saying that if S takes something to be red, or blue, or green, or yellow, then it is evident to S that there is something that *is* red, or blue, or green, or yellow. This would also hold true for other sensible characteristics and relations.

Variants of Principle C have been proposed by A. Meinong and H. H. Price.[10] But where I have said that beliefs pertaining to the perception of sensible characteristics are beliefs in what is *evident*, Meinong

[10] See A. Meinong, *Über die Erfarhrungsgrundlagen unseres Wissens* (Berlin: Julius Springer, 1906); H. H. Price, *Perception* (New York: Robert M. McBride & Co., 1933), p. 185; Roderick M. Chisholm, *Perceiving: A Philosophical Study* (Ithaca: Cornell University Press, 1957), Chap. 6.

qualifies the principle by saying that such perception yields only "presumptive evidence" (*Vermutungsevidenz*) and Price says that it yields only "prima-facie evidence." There are two reasons for considering such a qualification.

We may wish to say, for one thing, that rules of evidence are like many rules of morality in that they are "defeasible" or capable of being "overridden." Some moral philosophers have held, for example, that promise-making, *as such* ("other things being equal"), requires promise-keeping, and yet that any particular instance of promise-making may occur as part of a larger situation which does *not* require promise-keeping (we know, say, that a great disaster would result if, on this particular occasion, the promise were kept); in such a case, the "prima-facie requirement" to keep the promise is *defeated* or *overridden* by the larger situation. To say, then, that there is an "absolute requirement" on any given occasion to keep the promise would be to say, first, that there is a prima-facie requirement to keep it, and secondly, that there is no larger situation which defeats or overrides this requirement. One might hold similarly, and possibly this is the view of Meinong and Price, that a perception may, as such, confer "prima-facie evidence" upon a given proposition (say, the proposition that S sees something to be yellow) and yet occur as part of a larger situation which, as such, does not confer "prima-facie evidence" upon that proposition (he sees the thing under lights which are such that it is reasonable for him to believe that white things seen under those lights will be mistaken for things that are yellow). If one were to hold this, then one could go on to say that a perception confers "absolute evidence" provided it confers "prima-facie evidence" and is not thus defeated or overriden by any larger situation. And then, to assess the "larger situation" on any occasion, one might appeal Carneades' "close scrutiny and test"; I believe, in fact, that this is the correct way of looking at the matter. For simplicity, however, let us proceed upon the assumption that our principles are not "defeasible." [11]

But there is still another reason for introducing the term "prima facie" and for withholding any unqualified application of the term "evident" to the perceptions we have been considering (and this additional reason will hold even if the larger situation passes Carneades' "close scrutiny and test"). It is possible for an *unveridical* perception to satisfy our tests and criteria. That is to say, from the fact that a man believes that he perceives something to have a certain characteristic, it will not follow that he does perceive anything to have that characteristic. Hence, if we say unqualifiedly that the perceptions countenanced

[11] For a more detailed discussion of this concept and some of its relations to the theory of knowledge, see Roderick M. Chisholm, "The Ethics of Requirement," *The American Philosophical Quarterly*, I (1964), 147-53.

by our principle are evident, we must say that there can be some propositions that are both evident and false.

It must be conceded that this situation confronts us with a dilemma. If we say that *no* proposition can be both evident and false, then we may be restricting the evident to those trivial propositions that we have called directly evident. And if we say that our knowledge extends beyond the directly evident, then we may be committed to saying that some things that are evident may be false (though not to saying that any proposition that we *know* to be true is false).

The second horn of this dilemma would seem to be the lesser of the two evils. If we say that it is possible for an evident proposition to be false, then we are able to assure ourselves that there are evident propositions about external physical things; we are also able to assure ourselves, with respect to any evident proposition, that if the proposition is false, it can be justified at least by what is true. But we cannot assure ourselves that every evident proposition is true. This conclusion is sometimes expressed paradoxically by saying that knowledge involves an element of "animal faith." [12] We shall return to this problem in the final chapter.

Memory   When Carneades sets out to establish "concurrence" and to "test and scrutinize" his perceptions, he makes use of certain independent information. Or more exactly, he appeals to certain beliefs that he has—beliefs about the properties of the things that he is perceiving, about the condition of the intervening medium, about his own psychological and physiological state. But he fails to tell us anything about the credentials of these independent beliefs. Clearly, this gap in his account should be filled by reference to *memory*.

The word "memory" presents us with a terminological difficulty analogous to that presented by "perception." Consider a case in which, as one might say, a man's memory has "deceived him": the man would have said, honestly and sincerely, that he remembered a certain event to have occurred; actually, the event did not occur at all. Such deceptions of memory are common; "we remember remembering things and later finding them to be false." [13] But if we say "what he remembered is false," the ordinary interpretation of the word "remember" will render

[12] We may say of the evident what J. M. Keynes said about probability: ". . . there is no direct relation between the truth of a proposition and its probability. Probability begins and ends with probability. That a scientific investigation pursued on account of its probability will generally lead to truth, rather than falsehood, is at best only probable. The proposition that a course of action guided by the most probable considerations will generally lead to success, is not certainly true and has nothing to recommend it but probability." *A Treatise on Probability* (London: Macmillan & Co., Ltd., 1921), p. 322.

[13] C. I. Lewis, *An Analysis of Knowledge and Valuation* (La Salle, Ill.: Open Court Publishing Co., 1946), p. 334.

what we say contradictory; hence, if we wish to take "remember" in this ordinary way, we must express the fact in question by saying, "What he *thought* he remembered is false." And of those cases where one's memory is not thus deceptive, we may say that "what he thought he remembered is true."

Since both memory and perception are capable of playing us false, we run a twofold risk when we appeal to the memory of a perception. Let us suppose that Mr. S defends his claim to know "A cat was on the roof" by saying he thinks he remembers having perceived one there. The situation presents us with four possibilities. (1) The present memory and the past perception are both veridical: he did think he perceived a cat and what he saw was, in fact, a cat. (2) He correctly remembers having thought he saw a cat; but what he saw was not a cat. In this case, the fault lies with the past perception and not with the present memory. (3) He incorrectly remembers having thought he saw a cat; but what he really thought he saw, at the time, was a squirrel, and in fact it was a squirrel that he saw. In this case, the fault lies with the present memory and not with the past perception. (4) He incorrectly remembers having thought he saw a cat; but what he thought he saw, at the time, was a squirrel, and the perception was unveridical, for there was no squirrel there at all. In this case, the fault lies both with the present memory and the past perception. As we know, however, memory, by a kind of happy failure, if not an act of dishonesty, may correct the past perception: The man thought he saw a squirrel but it was in fact a cat, and now he thinks he remembers that he thought he saw a cat. Ordinary language provides us with no clear way of distinguishing these different types of deception, and memory is likely to receive more blame than it deserves. But it would seem to be clear, in general, that we should assign a lower degree of evidence to the deliverances of memory.

Where we said that one type of perceptual belief is *reasonable*, and another, *evident*, let us now say of the memories of such beliefs that they are *acceptable* and *reasonable*, respectively. We may add, then, the following two principles:

(D) If S believes that he remembers having perceived something to have a certain property F, then the proposition that he does remember having perceived something to be F, as well as the proposition that he perceived something to be F and the proposition that something was F, is *acceptable* for S.

(E) If there is a certain sensible characteristic F, such that S believes he remembers having perceived something to be F, then the proposition that he does remember having perceived something to be F, as well as the proposition that he perceived something to be F and the proposition that something was F, is *reasonable* for S.

Variants of these two principles have been suggested by other philosophers: Meinong held that our memory judgments, as he called them, possess "immediate presumptive evidence." Russell has said that every memory should "command a certain degree of credence." And Lewis said that "whatever is remembered, whether as explicit recollection or merely in the form of our sense of the past, is *prima-facie* credible because so remembered." [14]

There is still more that can be said in behalf of memory.

If our memories of sensible perceptions are reasonable, so, too, must be our memories of the "self-presenting states" discussed in the preceding chapter. If I think that I remembered that I believed, or desired, or hoped, or loved, or that I undertook a certain thing, or that I was appeared to in a certain way, then, for me, the statements expressing what I thus think that I remember are reasonable. Let us add, therefore:

(F)   If there is a "self-presenting state" such that S believes that he remembers having been in that state, then the proposition that he does remember having been in that state, as well as the proposition that he was in that state, is one that is *reasonable* for S.

We have said that our perception of things in motion, or at rest, and our perception of events in temporal succession are sources of what is evident. In saying this, we have conceded the evident character of "proteraesthesis," or our apprehension of the "immediate past." [15] Whenever we perceive a thing to be in motion, or to be at rest, and whenever we perceive a succession of events, as we do when we listen to a melody or to a conversation, we perceive one event as being temporally prior to another. When we do perceive one event as being temporally prior, then we perceive the former as being past. Whether this apprehension of the immediate past is to be called "memory" may be a matter only of terminology. But if we do call it "memory," then we may say that what we thus remember, or think we remember, is something that is *evident*.[16]

Hence, we have replaced Carneades' first thesis or principle, which

[14] A. Meinong, "*Zur erkenntnistheoretischen Würdigung des Gedächtnisses*," in *Gesammelte Abhandlungen* (Leipzig: Johann Ambrosius Barth, 1933), p. 207; first published in 1896. Bertrand Russell, *An Inquiry into Meaning and Truth* (New York: W. W. Norton & Co., Inc., 1940), pp. 192-202; C. I. Lewis, *An Analysis of Knowledge and Valuation*, p. 334.

[15] Franz Brentano uses the term "*Proterästhese*" in this connection; Russell uses "immediate past." See Brentano's *Die Lehre vom richtigen Urteil* (Bern: A. Francke, 1956), p. 158, and Russell's *Inquiry into Meaning and Truth*, p. 192.

[16] And if we call it "memory" we should not cease to call it "perception." "Hearing one note to precede another" may not be analyzed into "Hearing the one note and subsequently hearing another" or into "Remembering one note and hearing another."

states that all of our "perceptions" are acceptable, by several different theses about perception and memory. In one respect, as we have noted, our several theses are epistemically more rigorous than was the first thesis of Carneades. For if we follow the account of Carneades that has been handed down to us, we may be required to say that, for Mr. S, "There is a thief in the garden" may express a perception and hence be acceptable. But we have suggested a way in which what is expressed by "There is a thief in the garden" may be excluded from the perceptions that are to be taken as initially acceptable. In another respect, our several theses are epistemically more lenient than the first thesis of Carneades. For they allow us to say of certain types of propositions not only that such propositions are acceptable, but also that they are reasonable, and that some of them—those that pertain to sensible characteristics and relations—are evident.

But our principles do not yet allow us to say, of Mr. S, that it is evident to him that a cat is on the roof.

We must return, then, to the concept of *confirmation*.

Confirmation and concurrence   Unfortunately, the logic of induction has not yet been developed to the point where it is possible to say what it means for one proposition to *confirm*, or to *lend support to*, another. We may say, of course, that the premises of a good inductive argument confirm or lend support to the conclusion, and we can identify many good inductive arguments as well as many bad ones. Let us assume, in what follows, that we have sufficient understanding of the concept of confirmation to be able to use it in connection with our present problem.

First, we may expand the class of propositions that our principles are to countenance as being acceptable for S.

Since whatever is evident is also reasonable and since whatever is reasonable is also acceptable, we may say that all of the propositions countenanced by principles A through F are acceptable. It will be convenient to say of the propositions so countenanced that they are all *empirically acceptable* for S. We may now apply the concept of confirmation and say that whatever is confirmed or supported by the set of all of those propositions that are empirically acceptable, is itself acceptable.[17] Hence, we may add the following to our principles:

[17] Strictly speaking, our definition of "empirically acceptable" should be qualified. Consider the set of propositions countenanced by principles A through F; then subtract from that set any self-contradictory propositions and any pairs of propositions that contradict each other (we may hope, but we have no real assurance, that our set includes no such propositions). The result will be the set of propositions that are empirically acceptable. It is essential that this set contain no contradictions, for otherwise it could be said to confirm, or lend support to, any proposition whatever.

(G) If *h* is confirmed by the set of all those propositions *e*, such that *e* is empirically acceptable for *S* at *t*, then *h* is *acceptable* for *S* at *t*.

The class of acceptable propositions may now include a vast number of inductive hypotheses and will thus go considerably beyond the content of memory and perception. *S*'s acceptable memory propositions will include various propositions about cats and roofs; possibly, therefore, the inductive hypotheses admitted by Principle G will include generalizations about cats and roofs, for such generalizations may be confirmed by what *S* thinks that he perceives and remembers.

Next, by applying Carneades' concept of *concurrence* to this expanded class of acceptable propositions, we are also able to expand the class of propositions that are to be countenanced as being *reasonable*. When Carneades said that a group of presentations might be concurrent, he meant that each member of the group would support, and also be supported by, the other members of the group. Perhaps the concept of concurrence can be explicated like this: Any set of propositions that are mutually consistent and logically independent of each other (no one logically implies another) is *concurrent* provided that each member of the set is confirmed by the conjunction of all the other members of the set.[18]

There will conceivably be many sets of concurrent propositions among the propositions that are now acceptable for *S*. Let us consider, then, the following principle:

(H) If *h* is a member of a set of concurrent propositions, each of which is acceptable for *S* at *t*, then *h* is *reasonable* for *S* at *t*.

In other words, if among the propositions that are acceptable there is a set of propositions related by mutual support, then each of the propositions so related is also reasonable.

The following is an example, slightly oversimplified, of what might be such a concurrent set: "There is a cat on the roof today; there was one there yesterday; there was one there the day before yesterday; there was one there the day before that; and there is a cat on the roof almost every day." We may assume that the first statement expresses a present perception, and therefore, that it expresses what is reasonable (hence, also acceptable) by Principle B; we may assume that the second, third, and fourth statements express certain memories, and therefore, that they express what is acceptable by Principle D; and we may assume that the final statement is confirmed by the set of all of those state-

---

[18] Cf. the definition of "coherence" in H. H. Price's *Perception*, p. 183, and the definition of "congruence" in C. I. Lewis' *An Analysis of Knowledge and Valuation*, p. 338; Lewis discusses the logical properties of this concept in detail. I am indebted to Charles Raff for correcting an earlier definition of "concurrence."

ments that are empirically acceptable for S, and therefore, that it expresses what is acceptable by Principle G. Each of the five propositions thus formulated may be said to be confirmed by the set of all the others. They are mutually consistent, hence, they are concurrent; and therefore, they are all reasonable by Principle H.

Carneades had spoken of concurring presentations as hanging together like "links in a chain." But Meinong's figure may be more illuminating: "One may think of playing-cards. No one of them, uncreased, is capable of standing by itself, but several of them, leaned against each other, can serve to hold each other up." [19] Each of the propositions in our concurrent set must be acceptable on its own if we are to derive reasonability from concurrence, just as each of the members of a house of cards must have its own degree of substance and rigidity if the house is not to collapse. (We may be reluctant to compare reasonability with a house of cards. In this event, Meinong has two other figures for us: the arch of a bridge, and a stack of weapons in the field.)

And finally, from our concurrent set of propositions—now reasonable as well as acceptable—we extract still another class of propositions; the members of this new class will be countenanced as being evident. We will say, in short, that every perceptual proposition belonging to such a concurrent set is evident.

(I)   If S believes at t that he perceives something to have a certain property F, if h is the proposition that there is something having that property F, and if h is a member of a set of concurrent propositions each of which is acceptable for S at t, then h is *evident* to S at t.

The set of concurrent propositions cited just above includes the perceptual proposition "A cat is on the roof." Hence, in virtue of Principle I, and our earlier definition of knowledge, we may be able to say, at last, that S *knows* that there is a cat on the roof.

Here, then, we have a sketch of a theory of empirical evidence.[20]

[19] A. Meinong, *Über Möglichkeit und Wahrscheinlichkeit* (Leipzig: Johann Ambrosius Barth, 1915), p. 465.

[20] A complete theory of empirical evidence would also deal with this question: Under what conditions, if any, would confirmation by a set of evident propositions make another proposition evident? It would be absurd to suppose that whenever we find that a given hypothesis is more probable than not in relation to our evidence, we are then justified in adding that hypothesis to our evidence and using it as a basis for additional inductions. The set of premises (e) that Jones is one of the Christians in Goleta, that 51 of the 100 Christians in Goleta are Protestants, and that 26 of the Protestants there are Presbyterians could be said to make it probable (h) that Jones is a Protestant, for h is more probable than not in relation to e. If now we add h to our evidence, our increased evidence base will then make it probable (i) that Jones is a Presbyterian. But under these conditions it would be absurd to widen our evidence base still further and count "Jones is a Presbyterian" as a proposition that is evident. Yet it is often presupposed in writings on the philosophy

Corrections of detail may well be required; but it is only by means of *some* such principles as these that we can say that what is indirectly evident is "known through" what is directly evident. Principle A refers to every "self-presenting state," and thus to everything that is directly evident. Principles B and C apply to premises stating what S thinks he perceives; and principles D, E, and F apply to premises stating what S thinks he remembers. As we have seen, if S thinks that he perceives that something *a* has a certain property F, or if he thinks he remembers that *a* was F, then it is directly evident to him that he does think he perceives that *a* is F, or that he does think that he remembers that *a* was F. Principles G, H, and I refer to certain logical relations holding among the propositions countenanced by the principles; and these principles may be satisfied even if S does not know that they are satisfied. Hence, we may say that we have a set of principles enabling us to derive some of the things that are indirectly evident from what is directly evident.

Are there other types of knowledge for which our principles should be adequate? How are we to decide?

---

of science that there are some conditions under which confirmation by a set of evident propositions can thus confer evidence upon a proposition that the set does not entail. An unsolved "problem of induction" is that of saying just what these conditions might be.

THE PROBLEM

OF THE CRITERION

4

Two   Two quite different questions of the theory of knowledge are
questions   "*What* do we know?" and "How are we to decide, in any particular case, *whether* we know?" The first of these may also be put by asking "What is the *extent* of our knowledge?" and the second, by asking "What are the *criteria* of knowing?"

If we know the answer to either one of these questions, then, perhaps, we may devise a procedure that will enable us to answer the other. If we can specify the criteria of knowledge, we may have a way of deciding how far our knowledge extends. Or if we know how far it does extend, and are able to say what the things are that we know, then we may be able to formulate criteria enabling us to mark off the things that we do know from those that we do not.

But if we do not have the answer to the first question, then, it would seem, we have no way of answering the second. And if we do not have the answer to the second, then, it would seem, we have no way of answering the first.

It is characteristic of "empiricism" (but not only of "empiricism") to assume that we have an answer to the second of these two questions and then to attempt to answer the first on the basis of the answer to the second. *Experience,* in one or another of its various senses, is said to be the source of our knowledge; every valid claim to knowledge, it is supposed, will satisfy certain *empirical* criteria; and these criteria, it is then concluded, may be used to determine the extent of our knowledge. Empiricism thus begins paradoxically with a general premise. But if Hume is right, a consistent application of these criteria indicates that we know next to nothing about ourselves and about the physical objects around us.

Hence, it is characteristic of "commonsensism," as an alternative tradition in the theory of knowledge, to assume that we do know most, if not all, of those things that ordinary people think that they know. G. E. Moore has written: "There is no reason why we should not, in this respect, make our philosophical opinions agree with what we necessarily believe at other times. There is no reason why I should not confidently assert that I do really *know* some external facts, although I cannot prove the assertion except by simply assuming that I do. I am, in fact, as certain of this as of anything; and as reasonably certain of it." [1] If we take this point of view, then we can say, with Thomas Reid, that if empiricism has the consequence that we do not know any of these "external facts," then empiricism, *ipso facto*, is false.

A third point of view, with respect to our pair of questions, is that of "scepticism" or "agnosticism." The sceptic or agnostic does *not* assume at the outset that he has an answer to the first question or that he has an answer to the second. Thus, he is able to conclude: "We do not know what, if anything, we know, and we have no way of deciding, in any particular case, whether or not we know."

Many philosophers, perhaps unwittingly, have taken all three points of view. Thus, a single philosopher may attempt to set out in three different directions at once. First, he will employ what he takes to be his knowledge of external physical things in order to test the adequacy of various possible criteria of knowing; in this case, he begins with a claim to know and not with a criterion. Second, he will employ what he takes to be an adequate criterion of knowing in order to decide whether he knows anything about "other minds"; in this case, he begins with a criterion and not with a claim to know. And third, he will approach the field of ethics without either type of preconception; he will not begin with a criterion and he will not begin with a claim to know. Therefore, he will not arrive at any criterion or at any claim to know.

"Sources" of knowledge One approach to the question "How are we to decide, in any particular case, *whether* we know?" is to refer to the "sources" of our knowledge and to say that an ostensible item of knowledge is genuine if, and only if, it is the product of a properly accredited source. Thus, it is traditional in Western philosophy to say that there are four such sources:

1. "external perception"
2. memory
3. "self-awareness" ("reflection," or "inner consciousness")
4. reason

[1] *Philosophical Studies* (London: Routledge & Kegan Paul, Ltd., 1922), p. 163.

("Self-awareness" pertains to what we have been calling the directly evident; and "reason" is said to be that by means of which we have our a priori knowledge of necessity.)

Descartes wrote, for example, that "in the matter of the cognition of facts two things alone have to be considered, ourselves who know and the objects themselves which are to be known. Within us there are four faculties only which we can use for this purpose, viz., understanding, imagination, sense, and memory. . . ." [2] And Thomas Reid said, even more clearly: "Thus the faculties of consciousness, of memory, of external sense, and of reason are all equally the gifts of nature. No good reason can be assigned for receiving the testimony of one of them, which is not of equal force with regard to the others." [3]

The principles of evidence that we have tried to formulate may be looked upon as an acknowledgment of the first three, at least, of these traditional sources. The sentence "I think I perceive that thing to be so and so" expresses the content of self-awareness. But we stated conditions under which thinking that one perceives something to be so and so may be said to confer evidence or reasonableness upon the proposition that something *is* so and so; in so doing, we acknowledged *perception* as a source of knowing. "I think I remember having perceived that thing to be so and so" also expresses the content of self-awareness. But we stated conditions under which thinking that one remembers having perceived something to be so and so might be said to confer reasonableness or acceptability upon the proposition that something *was* so and so; in so doing, we acknowledged *memory* as a source of knowing. And we have said that the content of *self-awareness* is directly evident.

But the appeal to such "sources" leaves us with a kind of puzzlement. If the question "How are we to decide, in any particular case, whether we know?" is seriously intended, then the reply "An ostensible item of knowledge is genuine if, and only if, it is the product of a properly accredited source of knowledge" is not likely to be sufficient. For such a reply naturally leads to further questions: "How are we to decide whether an ostensible source of knowledge *is* properly accredited?" and "How are we to decide just *what* it is that is yielded by a properly accredited source of knowledge?"

Let us now consider how this general "problem of the criterion" arises in particular cases.

[2] "Rules for the Direction of the Mind," in *The Philosophical Works of Descartes*, I, ed. E. S. Haldane and G. R. Ross (London: Cambridge University Press, 1934), p. 35.

[3] *Essays on the Intellectual Powers*, Essay VI, Chap. 4, in *The Works of Thomas Reid*, 4th ed., ed. Sir William Hamilton (London: Longmans, Green & Company, Ltd., 1854), p. 439.

"Knowledge of right and wrong" as one example At the risk of some slight oversimplification, let us begin with one of the controversial questions of moral philosophy. Do we know any distinctively *moral,* or *ethical,* facts? Or what is the status of the claim to such knowledge? The controversies that such questions involve present us with a pattern that recurs with respect to every disputed area of knowledge.

"Mercy as such is good" and "Ingratitude as such is bad" are examples of distinctively moral, or ethical, sentences. It has been held that these sentences express something that we can know to be true; it has also been held that they do not. The controversy that concerns us here arises only after the following point has been agreed upon—namely, that if we start from the kind of empirical fact that we have been considering up to now, we cannot construct either a good deductive argument or a good inductive argument to support such statements as "Mercy as such is good" and "Ingratitude as such is bad." Proceeding from this fact, let us contrast the positions of the moral "intuitionist" (or "dogmatist") and the moral "sceptic" (or "agnostic").

The "intuitionist" will reason in essentially the following way:

(P)   We have knowledge of certain ethical facts.
(Q)   Experience and reason do not yield such knowledge.
▶ (R)   There is an additional source of knowledge.

The "sceptic," finding no such additional source of knowledge, reasons with equal cogency in the following way:

(Not–R)   There is no source of knowledge other than experience and reason.
(Q)   Experience and reason do not yield any knowledge of ethical facts.
▶ (Not–P)   We do not have knowledge of any ethical facts.

The intuitionist and the sceptic agree with respect to the second premise, which states that reason and experience do not yield any knowledge of ethical facts. The intuitionist, however, takes as his first premise the contradictory of the sceptic's conclusion; and the sceptic takes as *his* first premise the contradictory of the intuitionist's conclusion. We could say, therefore, that the sceptic begins with a philosophical generalization ("There is no source of knowledge other than experience and reason") and concludes by denying, with respect to a certain type of fact, or alleged fact, that we have knowledge of that type of fact. The intuitionist, on the other hand, begins by saying that we do have knowledge of the type of fact in question and he concludes by denying the sceptic's philosophical generalization. How is one to choose between the two approaches?

The logic of the two arguments reminds us that there is still another possibility. For if P and Q imply R, then not only do Not-R and Q imply Not-P, but also Not-R and P imply Not-Q. Hence, one could also argue in this way:

(Not–R)   There is no source of knowledge other than experience and reason.

(P)   We have knowledge of certain ethical facts.

▶ (Not–Q)   Experience and reason yield knowledge of ethical facts.

The first premise of this new argument is rejected by the intuitionist and accepted by the sceptic; the second premise is rejected by the sceptic and accepted by the intuitionist; and the conclusion is rejected by both the intuitionist and the sceptic.

With this third type of argument, one might be said to reject the *faculty* that is claimed by the intuitionist and yet to accept the intuitionist's claim to *knowledge*; in so doing, one is led to reject the *assessment* of experience and reason common to the intuitionist and the sceptic. This is the only possible procedure for one who believes that we do have knowledge of ethical facts and that we do not have a special faculty of moral intuition.

But any such procedure leaves us with a Kantian question: In view of the nature of experience and reason, *how* is such ethical knowledge possible? If we cannot derive the propositions of ethics by applying deduction or induction to the kinds of empirical propositions that we have considered up to now, what is the sense in which experience and reason may yet be said to "yield" our ethical knowledge? There are, I believe, only two possible answers.

One of these may be called "reductive." If we approach the problem "reductively," we attempt to show that the sentences purporting to express our ethical knowledge ("Mercy as such is good" and "Ingratitude as such is bad") can be *translated* or paraphrased into empirical sentences that more obviously express the deliverances of experience. Perhaps we will say that "Mercy as such is good" really means the same as "I approve of mercy," or "Most of the people in our culture circle approve of mercy" or "Merciful actions tend to make people happy." But these attempted reductions are entirely implausible; the sentences expressing our ostensible ethical knowledge *seem* at least to express considerably more than is expressed by any of their ostensible empirical translations.

The other type of answer might be called "critical cognitivism." If we take this approach, we will not say that there are empirical sentences that might serve as translations of the sentences expressing our ethical knowledge; but we will say that there are empirical truths which *enable us to know* certain truths of ethics. Or to use our earlier expression, we will say that the truths of ethics are "known through" certain facts of experience. The latter will then be said to be *signs*, or *criteria*, of the ethical truths. The evil of ingratitude, for example, does not lie in the fact that I happen to detest it; but the fact that I happen to detest it, or at least the fact that I happen to detest it under certain conditions that can be identified, serves to make known to me the fact that ingratitude *is* something that is evil. My own feeling is a *sign* of the evil nature of ingratitude, and so it could be said to *confer evidence upon* the statement that ingratitude is evil. This point of view is typical of "value-theory" in the Austrian tradition, where our feeling for what is valuable, *das Wertgefühle*, is said to be something we know by means of our "inner consciousness," as well as that which makes known to us what is valuable and what is not.

"Critical cognitivism" will hardly be acceptable to the intuitionist or the sceptic, but there are two points to be made in its favor, the first being that it is a consequence of premises, each of which, when taken separately, seems to be acceptable, if not reasonable. For the critical cognitivist may well say: "We do know that mercy is good and that ingratitude is bad. The sentences in which such truths are expressed are not inductive or deductive consequences of sentences expressing our perceptions, our memories of our perceptions, or our own psychological states; nor can they be translated or paraphrased into such sentences. Yet we have no moral intuitions; experience and reason are our only sources of knowledge. Hence, there must be some empirical truths which serve to make known the facts of ethics. And these truths can only be those that pertain to our feelings for what is good and what is evil."

There is a second point that the "critical cognitivist" may make. He may remind us that the analogue of his critical cognitivism is the most reasonable approach to another, less controversial, area of knowledge. He will be referring to our knowledge of external, physical things —for example, to our knowledge, on a particular occasion, that a cat is on the roof.

'Knowledge of external things" as another example

We have seen that from directly evident premises—premises expressing our "self-awareness"—neither induction nor deduction will yield the conclusion "A cat is on the roof." There are at least four different ways in which we might react to this fact. (1) The "intuitionist" will conclude that we have still another source of knowledge, namely, that we know external things not through our "self-presenting states," but by means of some other type of experience. But no such experience is to be found. (2) The "sceptic" will infer that we cannot know, on any occasion, that a cat is on the roof. But we know that he is mistaken. (3) The "reductionist" will infer that "A cat is on the roof" can be translated or paraphrased into sentences expressing one's self-awareness—more particularly, into sentences about the ways in which one is appeared to. To see the implausibility of the reductivist point of view, we have only to ask ourselves *what* appearance sentences —what sentences of the form "I am appeared to in such and such a way"—could possibly express what it is that we know when we know that a cat is on the roof.[4] (4) And the "critical cognitivist" will take the course we tried to sketch in the preceding chapter. He will say that there are principles of evidence, other than the principles of induction and deduction, which will tell us, for example, under what conditions the state we have called "thinking that one perceives" will *confer evidence*, or *confer reasonableness*, upon propositions about external things; and they will tell us under what conditions that state we have called "thinking that one remembers" will *confer reasonableness*, or *confer acceptability*, upon propositions about the past.[5]

"Other minds"   Another version of the problem of the criterion concerns our knowledge of "other minds." Each of us knows various things about the thoughts, feelings, and purposes of other people; we may be able to say, for example, "I know that Jones is thinking about a horse" or "I know that he is feeling somewhat depressed." Perhaps we will justify our claims to such knowledge by reference, in part, to our perception of certain physical facts which we take to manifest or express the thoughts and feelings in question ("I can see it in his eyes and in the way in which he clenches his teeth, and I can hear it in the sound

---

[4] The principal difficulty standing in the way of "phenomenalism" (the technical term for this type of reductionism) may be traced to perceptual relativity—to the fact that the ways in which a thing will appear depend not only upon the properties of the thing, but also upon the conditions under which it is perceived and upon the state of the perceiver. Since it is the joint operation of the things we perceive with the conditions under which we perceive them that determines the ways in which the things will appear, we cannot correlate any group of appearances with any particular physical fact (say, a cat being on the roof) unless we refer to some *other* physical fact—the state of the medium and of the perceiver. Trying to define the particular physical fact by reference to appearances alone is not unlike trying to define "uncle" in terms of "descendent" alone and without the use of "male" or "female." For further details, see C. I. Lewis, "Professor Chisholm and Empiricism," *Journal of Philosophy*, XLV (1948), 517-24; Roderick Firth, "Radical Empiricism and Perceptual Relativity," *Philosophical Review*, LIX (1950), 164-83, 319-31; and Roderick M. Chisholm, *Perceiving: A Philosophical Study* (Ithaca: Cornell University Press, 1957), pp. 189-97. The three articles cited are reprinted in *Perceiving, Sensing, and Knowing*, ed. Robert J. Swartz (Garden City: Doubleday & Company, Inc., 1965).

[5] See principles B, C, D, and E, concerning "reasonableness," in the preceding chapter.

of his voice"); or we may even justify them by reference to our own feeling of V*erstehen,* or "intuitive understanding" (". . . we know a creature's angry by the way we have felt when we have acted rather as he is acting.") [6] The philosopher may then ask: What justification is there for believing that if a man looks and acts in such and such a way or if he leaves me with such and such a feeling then he is either thinking about a horse or he is feeling somewhat depressed?

It is common to suppose that such knowledge is yielded by the traditional "sources" listed above. We know about the thoughts and feelings of other people, it is supposed, in virtue of the knowledge that is yielded by (1) our perception of external things, and in particular, our perception of our own bodies and of the bodies of other people, (2) our immediate awareness of our own thoughts and feelings, (3) our memories of things we come to know by means of such perceptions and states of awareness, and (4) the application of "reason" to the things that we know in these various ways. But how, precisely, can this material be made to yield any knowledge of the thoughts and feelings of other people?

One may be tempted to answer this question by appealing to an enumerative induction. "More often than not, when a man makes a gesture of such and such a sort, he is feeling depressed; this man is now making a gesture of that sort; therefore, in all probability, he is depressed." Or, "More often than not, when Jones rides by those fields he is reminded of the horse that he once owned; he is riding by them now and has a look of fond recollection in his eye; therefore, in all probability, he is thinking about his horse again." But this type of answer obviously does not solve our philosophical problem. For the instances to which we appeal when we make our induction ("He made this gesture yesterday when he was depressed" or "The last time he was here he thought about a horse") presuppose the general type of knowledge-claim we are now trying to justify ("What is your justification for thinking you know that he *was* depressed yesterday?" or "What is your justification for thinking you know that he *was* thinking about a horse that day?")

If we are not to presuppose the type of knowledge-claim that we are trying to justify, then our argument must be an instance of "hypothetical induction." The "hypothesis" that Jones is now depressed, or that he is thinking about a horse, will be put forward as the most likely explanation of certain other things we know—presumably, certain facts about Jones's present behavior and demeanor. But in order to construct an inductive argument in which the hypothesis that Jones is depressed,

[6] The second quotation is from John Wisdom, *Other Minds* (Oxford: Basil Blackwell, 1952), p. 194.

or that he is thinking about a horse, *is* thus to be confirmed, we must have access to a premise telling us what some of the consequences of Jones's depression, or some of the consequences of his thinking about a horse, are likely to be. And how are we to justify *this* premise if we are not entitled to make use of any information about Jones's depression or thoughts?

The only possible way of finding the premise that our hypothetical induction thus requires is to appeal to still another induction—this time an argument from analogy. (Those who argue that there is life on Venus appeal to the "positive analogy" between Venus and the earth —the properties the two planets have in common. Those who argue that there is no life on Venus appeal to the "negative analogy"—the respects in which the two planets differ.) Thus, we might argue: "Jones and I have such and such physical characteristics in common; usually, as a result of being depressed, I will speak in such and such a tone of voice; therefore, in all probability, if Jones is depressed he will also speak in that tone of voice; he *is* speaking in that tone of voice." Or we might argue: "Jones and I have such and such physical characteristics in common; most of the time, when I think about a horse, I will say 'Yes' if stimulated by the words 'Are you thinking about a horse?' therefore, in all probability, Jones's thinking about a horse would predispose *him* to say 'Yes' if he were stimulated by the words 'Are you thinking about a horse?' and Jones, having been stimulated by those words, *does* say 'Yes.' " We are supposing that the first premise in each of these arguments appeals to a certain positive analogy obtaining between Jones and me. But we must not forget that whoever Jones may be, there is also an impressive negative analogy—difference in background, environment, heredity, physique, and general physiology—and that one could go on *ad indefinitum* enumerating such differences. If we are not entitled to begin with premises referring to Jones's states of mind, it will be very difficult indeed to assess the relative importance of the various points of analogy and disanalogy. Any such analogical argument, therefore, is certain to be weak. But we are supposing it is only by means of such an analogical argument that we can justify one of the premises of the hypothetical induction we now proceed to make (the premise stating "If Jones is depressed, he will speak in such and such a tone of voice" or "If Jones is thinking about a horse he will say 'Yes' if stimulated by 'Are you thinking about a horse?' "). Our hypothetical induction, in turn, will yield "Jones is depressed now" or "Jones is thinking about a horse" as being the most likely diagnosis of Jones's present behavior and demeanor.

However, if this procedure is the best that we have, then there is very little, if anything, that we can be said to *know* about the states of mind of other people.

And this fact leads us, once again, to the characteristic argument of the "intuitionist." Perception, memory, and "self-awareness," he will tell us, do not suffice to justify what it is that we claim to know about the states of mind of other people, for no deductive or inductive argument based upon the data of perception, memory, and "self-awareness" will warrant any claim to such knowledge; hence, there must be another source—possibly the V*erstehen,* or "intuitive understanding," of German philosophy and psychology.[7] The intuitionist's point would not be merely that in V*erstehen,* or intuitive understanding, we have a fruitful source of hypotheses about the mental states of other people (presumably there is no one who doubts the practical utility of this faculty); the intuitionist's point would pertain to justification. Thus, he might hold, for example, that the fact that a statement expresses one's V*erstehen* will confer reasonableness upon that statement.

The "intuitionist," then, will reason as he did in moral philosophy:

(Q)   We have knowledge of the states of mind of other people (for example, I know that Jones is thinking about a horse).

(R)   Such knowledge is not yielded by perception, memory, or "self-awareness."

(P)   Therefore, there is still another source of knowledge.

The three statements constituting this argument also yield the "sceptical" argument of the philosophical behaviorist:

(Not–R)   There is no source of knowledge other than perception, memory, and "self-awareness."

(Q)   Knowledge of the states of mind of other people is not yielded by perception, memory, or "self-awareness."

▶ (Not–P)   We do not have knowledge of the states of mind of other people.[8]

---

[7] The emphasis upon V*erstehen* as a source of knowledge may be traced to Wilhelm Dilthey's *Einleitung in die Geisteswissenschaften* (Leipzig: Tuebner, 1883), and to the writings of Max Scheler; see Alfred Schuetz, "Scheler's Theory of Intersubjectivity," *Philosophy and Phenomenological Research,* II (1942), 323-41.

[8] Cf. J. B. Watson, *The Ways of Behaviorism* (New York: W. W. Norton & Company, Inc., 1928), pp. 3, 7: "The behaviorist has nothing to say of 'consciousness.' How can he? Behaviorism is a natural science. He has neither seen, smelled, nor tasted consciousness nor found it taking part in any human reactions. How can he talk about it until he finds it in his path. . . . Behaviorism's challenge to introspective psychology was: 'You say there is such a thing as consciousness, that consciousness goes on in you—then prove it. You say that you have sensations, perceptions, and images—then demonstrate them as other sciences demonstrate their facts.' " The consistent behaviorist, of course, would also attempt to avoid the facts of "self-awareness."

As in the dispute about moral philosophy, the intuitionist and the sceptic agree with respect to the second premise; the intuitionist takes as his first premise the contradictory of the sceptic's conclusion; and the sceptic takes as *his* first premise the contradictory of the intuitionist's conclusion. There is one more possibility:

(Not–R)   There is no source of knowledge other than perception, memory, and "self-awareness."

(P)   We have knowledge of the states of mind of other people (for example, I know that Jones is thinking about a horse).

▶ (Not–Q)   Perception, memory, and "self-awareness" yield this knowledge.

Once again, we are presented with the question *"How* do perception, memory, and inner consciousness yield this knowledge?" and as before, we may choose between two answers.

The "reductivist" will tell us that sentences ostensibly concerning the thoughts and feelings of other people ("Jones is thinking about a horse") can be translated or paraphrased into sentences about the bodies of these people. But "reductivism" is no more plausible here than it was in the other cases. To see that this is so, we have only to ask ourselves: *What* sentences about Jones's body could possibly express what it is that we know when we know that Jones is thinking about a horse?

And the "critical cognitivist" will tell us that there are things we can know about a man's body and his behavior that will confer evidence, or reasonableness, upon propositions about these thoughts and feelings; he may add, in deference to *Verstehen,* that certain mental states of our own, which come into being when we are in the presence of others, confer reasonableness, or acceptability, upon propositions about the thoughts and feelings of others.

According to Thomas Reid's version of critical cognitivism, "certain features of the countenance, sounds of the voice, and gestures of the body, indicate certain thoughts and dispositions of mind." Reid's view is, in part, a view about the genesis of our knowledge (he refers, for example, to the way in which children acquire their beliefs). But it is also a theory of evidence—an account of what it is that confers evidence upon statements about other minds—and as such, it is worth quoting in detail:

> "When we see the sign, and see the thing signified always conjoined with it, experience may be the instructor, and teach us how that sign is to be interpreted. But how shall experience instruct us when we see the sign only, when the thing signified is invisible? Now, this is the case here: the thoughts and passions of the mind, as well as the mind

itself, are invisible, and therefore their connection with any sensible sign cannot be first discovered by experience; there must be some earlier source of this knowledge. Nature seems to have given to men a faculty or sense, by which this connection is perceived. And the operation of this sense is very analogous to that of the external senses.

"When I grasp an ivory ball in my hand, I feel a certain sensation of touch. In the sensation there is nothing external, nothing corporeal. The sensation is neither round nor hard; it is an act of feeling of mind, from which I cannot by reasoning, infer the existence of any body. But, by the constitution of my nature, the sensation carries along with it the conception and belief of a round hard body really existing in my hand. In like manner, when I see the features of an expressive face, I see only figure and colour variously modified. But by the constitution of my nature, the visible object brings along with it the conception and belief of a certain passion or sentiment in the mind of the person.

"In the former case, a sensation of touch is the sign, and the hardness and roundness of the body I grasp is signified by that sensation. In the latter case, the features of the person is the sign, and the passion or sentiment is signified by it." [9]

A final example Knowledge, or ostensible knowledge, of God and of what some take to be theological truths, provides us with a final illustration of the problem of the criterion. Perhaps we are now in a position to understand the type of impasse to which the various possible points of view give rise; therefore, perhaps we can express these points of view much more simply than any of their proponents can.

The "dogmatist" or "intuitionist" will argue that (P) we do have knowledge of the existence of God and of other theological facts; but (Q) this knowledge is not yielded, or significantly confirmed by, anything that is yielded by reason or experience; hence, (R) there is a source of knowledge in addition to reason and experience. Thus, Hugh of St. Victor held, in the twelfth century, that in addition to the *oculis carnis*, by means of which we know the physical world, and the *oculis rationis*, by means of which we know our own states of mind, there is also an *oculis contemplationis*, by means of which we know the truth of religion.[10]

Finding no such contemplative eye, the "agnostic"—the religious

---

[9] *Essays on the Intellectual Powers of Man*, Essay VI, Chap. 5, in *The Works of Thomas Reid*, pp. 449-50. Of the types of "sign" distinguished in the first two sentences of this passage, the stoics called the first "commemorative" and the second "indicative"; Sextus Empiricus, as a sceptic, held that there are no "indicative signs." See Sextus Empiricus, *Against the Logicians*, Book II, Chap. 3, in Vol. II of *Sextus Empiricus*, The Loeb Classical Library (Cambridge: Harvard University Press, 1933), pp. 313-97.

[10] See Maurice De Wulf, *History of Mediaeval Philosophy*, I (London: Longmans, Green & Company, Ltd., 1935), 214.

sceptic—argues that (Not-R) reason and experience are the only sources of knowledge; (Q) reason and experience do not supply any information, or significantly confirm any hypothesis, about the existence of God or about any other theological facts; hence, (Not-P) we have no knowledge about God.

And the third possibility is to argue that (Not-R) there is no source of knowledge other than experience and reason; (P) we have knowledge of the existence of God and of certain other theological facts; hence, (Not-Q) experience and reason do supply us with information about the existence of God and about other theological facts.

Before taking refuge in "reductionism" or "critical cognitivism," the theist may explore the possibilities of using induction and deduction in order to derive the truths in question from the deliverances of the *oculis carnis* and the *oculis rationis*. We will not try to evaluate the relative merits of (1) proving the existence of God from the facts of nature, (2) proving the existence of external things from the ways in which we are appeared to, and (3) proving the existence of other people's states of mind from facts about their behavior. But many theists who are not sceptics have doubts about the traditional proofs, and for them, the alternatives are "reductionism" and "critical cognitivism." [11]

"Reductionism" seems to be exemplified in contemporary Protestant theology. The cognitive content of such sentences as "God exists" is thought to be expressible in sentences about the thoughts, feelings, and behavior of religious people. To see the implausibility of reductionism, we have only to ask ourselves, as before: *What* sentences about the thoughts, feelings, and behavior of religious people can possibly express what it is that the religious man thinks he knows when he thinks he knows that God exists?

Finally, "critical cognitivism" would be the view that what we know about God is "known through" certain other things in precisely the way in which the content of other types of knowledge are "known through" the directly evident, or known through what is itself known through the directly evident. Just what the facts are that may be said to confer reasonableness, or acceptability, upon the ostensible truths of religion would seem to be problematic. But given such facts, whether they pertain to sacred writings, the sayings of religious teachers, or one's experience of "the holy," the critical cognitivist may distinguish, as theologians do, between *exegesis* and *hermeneutics*, the former being an account of just what these facts are, and the latter, an account of the types of proposition upon which they may be said to confer evidence, reasonableness, or acceptability. Our account of the directly evident in

[11] Cf. chaps. 2 and 6 in John Hick, *Philosophy of Religion*, Prentice-Hall Foundations of Philosophy Series.

Chapter 2 might similarly be said to be a matter of exegesis, and our account of the indirectly evident in Chapter 3, a matter of hermeneutics.

It may not be surprising, then, that the general problem of the criterion has created impasses in almost every branch of knowledge. I am afraid that I can throw no further light upon the problem itself; but if we can appreciate its difficulties, perhaps we will better understand some of the controversies that are involved in the topic of our next chapter—that type of knowledge that is said to be a priori. For there, too, philosophers are divided with respect to basic "criteriological" issues.

THE TRUTHS OF REASON

5

A traditional
view "There are also two kinds of truths: those of reasoning and those
of fact. The truths of reasoning are necessary, and their opposite is
impossible. Those of fact, however, are contingent, and their opposite is possible. When a truth is necessary, we can find the reason by
analysis, resolving the truth into simpler ideas and simpler truths until
we reach those that are primary." [Leibniz, *Monadology* 33]

"Reason," as we have noted, is sometimes said to function along
with "experience" as a "source" of knowledge. One traditional view of
the subject matter of the knowledge thus attributed to reason seems to
be based upon the assumptions that there is a valid distinction to be
drawn between properties and concrete individual things, or substances;
that there is an analogous distinction to be drawn between states of
affairs and concrete events; that properties may be related to each other
by entailment, or inclusion, and by exclusion; that states of affairs may
be similarly related; and that such relations hold necessarily. All of
these assumptions are properly said to be metaphysical.

This view also involves the epistemological assumption that in
certain instances, we can know that these relations hold, and that they
hold necessarily, and what is more, that we can know these truths of
reason a priori.

And finally, it involves the assumption that some of these truths
of reason are what constitute the subject matter of logic.

As in the other spheres of knowledge we have just considered,
there is also the possibility of scepticism—in the present case, scepticism
with respect to the "truths of reason." The apparent impasses that arise
between sceptic and nonsceptic, once again, are difficult, if not impossible, to remove. Some of those who are sceptical with respect to

metaphysics attempt to "reduce" the truths of reason to other, less objectionable truths; but these attempts at reduction seem to be no more plausible than those considered earlier.

Let us begin by attempting to sketch the metaphysical interpretation of these truths.

Inclusion and exclusion   Some properties (for example, that of being a horse, or being equine) are exemplified in several different individual things (for there are many different horses); other properties (for example, that of being perfectly round) are not exemplified in any individual thing; still other properties (for example, that of being the fastest runner) are exemplified in only one individual thing.

The relation of *entailment* or *inclusion* among properties is exemplified by these facts: The property of being square includes that of being rectangular, and that of being red includes that of being colored. The relation of *exclusion* is exemplified by these facts: The property of being square excludes that of being circular, and that of being red excludes that of being blue. To say that one property excludes another, therefore, is to say more than that the one fails to include the other. Being red fails to include being heavy, but it does not exclude being heavy; if it excluded being heavy, as it excludes being blue, then nothing could be both red and heavy.[1]

There are also compound properties—for example, that of being either red or blue, that of being both red and warm, that of being nonred, and that of being red-if-colored. Relations of inclusion and exclusion involving such properties may be illustrated in obvious ways: Being both red and square includes being red and excludes being circular; being both red and warm-if-red includes being warm; being both nonwarm and warm-if-red excludes being red.

Relations, on this view, may be thought of as being a kind of property. Among the properties of Socrates is that of being older than Plato, and hence, also that of being older than someone, as well as that of being older than anything that Plato is older than. Relations, like other properties, may be thought of as being themselves related by inclusion and exclusion. For example, bearing warmer-than to any particular thing x includes, and is included by, being borne cooler-than to by x; it also includes bearing warmer-than to whatever x bears warmer-than to, and it excludes being borne warmer-than to by x.

There are also certain more general truths about the relations of inclusion and exclusion. For example, every property F and every prop-

---

[1] "Being red excludes being blue" should not be taken to rule out the possibility of a thing being red in one part and blue in another; it tells us only that being red in one part at one time excludes being blue in exactly that same part at exactly that same time.

erty G is such that F's excluding G includes G's excluding F; F's excluding G includes F's including not-G; F excludes non-F, and includes F-or-G.

States of affairs (or to use a different terminology, possible states of affairs) are analogous to properties. Where a property may be exemplified in several different things, a state of affairs (for example, Socrates being in Athens) is exemplified in several different concrete events; other states of affairs (for example, Socrates being in Rome) are not exemplified in any concrete event. Still other states of affairs (for example, Socrates dying in 399 B.C.) are exemplified in only one concrete event.[2]

States of affairs, like properties, are related by inclusion and exclusion; for example, some men being Greeks includes, and is included by, some Greeks being men, and excludes no Greeks being men. States of affairs, like properties, may be compound; for example, some men being Greek and Plato being Roman; Socrates receiving inspiration being a sufficient condition for Socrates becoming a philosopher. Examples of relations of inclusion and exclusion involving compound states of affairs are: the conjunctive state of affairs, composed of (1) Socrates receiving inspiration and (2) Socrates receiving inspiration being a sufficient condition for Socrates becoming a philosopher, includes (3) Socrates becoming a philosopher; and the conjunctive state of affairs, composed of (1) Socrates not becoming a philosopher and (2) Socrates receiving inspiration being a sufficient condition for Socrates becoming a philosopher, excludes (3) Socrates receiving inspiration. These two examples are instances of more general truths: For every state of affairs, p and q, the conjunctive state of affairs, composed of p and of p being a sufficient condition of q, includes q; and the conjunctive state of affairs, composed of not-q and of p being a sufficient condition of q, excludes p. These latter "truths of reason" are thus said to be the kind of truth with which the logic of propositions is concerned.

And more generally, according to the present doctrine, when one sentence can be said necessarily to imply another, then the state of affairs intended by the one sentence includes the state of affairs intended by the other.

[2] There is no accepted uniform terminology for expressing this distinction. Where I have said "(possible) state of affairs" and "concrete events," others have said: "eternal object" and "occasion" (Whitehead); "states of affairs" and "space-time slabs of reality" (Lewis); and "generic propositions" and "individual propositions" (von Wright). Cf. A. N. Whitehead, *Science and the Modern World* (New York: The Macmillan Company, 1930), pp. 32-9; C. I. Lewis, *An Analysis of Knowledge and Valuation* (La Salle, Ill.: Open Court Publishing Co., 1946), pp. 52-55; and G. H. von Wright, *Norm and Action* (London: Routledge & Kegan Paul, Ltd., 1963), pp. 23-25. And where I said "properties," others have said "attributes," "essences," "meanings," "universals," or "intensions."

Knowledge of necessity is not a posteriori

When it is said that these truths of reason are known (or are capable of being known) "a priori," part of what is meant is that if they are known they are not known "a posteriori." A single example may suggest what is intended when it is said that these truths are not known a posteriori.

Corresponding to "Necessarily, being red excludes being blue," which is a truth about properties, the following general statement is a truth about individual things: "Necessarily, every individual thing, past, present, or future, is such that if it is red then it is not blue." If the latter truth were known a posteriori, then it would be justified by some induction or inductions; our evidence presumably would consist in the fact that a great variety of red things and a great variety of non-blue things have been observed in the past, and that up to now, no red things have been blue. We might thus inductively confirm "Every individual thing, past, present, or future, is such that if it is red then it is not blue"; we might then proceed to the further conclusion, "Necessarily, being red excludes being blue," and finally, to "Necessarily, every individual thing, past, present, or future, is such that if it is red then it is not blue."

Thus, there might be said to be three steps involved in an inductive justification of "Necessarily, being red excludes being blue": (1) the accumulation of instances—"This red thing is not blue," "That blue thing is not red," and so on—along with the summary statement "No red thing observed up to now has been blue"; (2) the inductive inference from these data to "Every individual thing, past, present, and future, is such that if it is red then it is not blue"; (3) the step from this inductive conclusion to "Necessarily, being red excludes being blue," and then to "Necessarily, every individual thing, past, present, or future, is such that if it is red then it is not blue."

Why *not* say that such "truths of reason" are thus known a posteriori?

For one thing, some of these truths pertain to properties that have never been exemplified. If we take "square," "rectangular," and "circular" in the precise way in which these words are usually interpreted in geometry, we must say that nothing is square, rectangular, or circular; things in nature, as Plato said, "fall short" of having such properties.[3] Hence, to justify "Necessarily, being square includes being rectangular and excludes being circular," we cannot even take the first of the three steps illustrated above; there being no squares, we cannot collect instances of squares that are rectangles and squares that are not circles.

For another thing, application of induction would seem to presuppose a knowledge of the "truths of reason." In setting out to confirm an

[3] *Phaedo*, 75a.

inductive hypothesis, we must be able to recognize what its consequences would be. Ordinarily, to recognize these we must apply deduction; we take the hypothesis along with other things that we know and we see what is then implied. All of this, it would seem, involves apprehension of truths of reason—such truths as may be suggested by "For every state of affairs, p and q, the conjunctive state of affairs, composed of p and of either not-p or q, includes q," and "All A's being B excludes some A's not being B." Hence, even if we are able to justify some of the "truths of reason" by inductive procedures, any such justification will presuppose others, and we will be left with some "truths of reason" which we have not justified by means of induction.[4]

And finally, the last of the three steps described above—the step from the inductive generalization "Every individual thing, past, present, and future, is such that if it is red then it is not blue" to "Necessarily, being red excludes being blue"—is not itself a matter of induction. This is best seen if we note that there are other inductive generalizations which obviously do not warrant a comparable step. Perhaps we are justified in saying, for example, "Every individual thing, past, present, and future, is such that if it is human then it does not live to be 200 years old" and "Every individual thing, past, present, and future, is such that if it is a quintuplet named 'Dionne' then it is not male." But these facts do not warrant the further conclusions "Necessarily, being human excludes being 200 years old" and "Necessarily, being a quintuplet named 'Dionne' excludes being male." Hence, the fact that we have justified the inductive generalization involved in the second of our three steps is not in itself sufficient to justify the necessary truth involved in the third.[5]

Thus, Kant said that *necessity* is a mark, or criterion, of the a priori.[6] If what we know is a necessary truth—if we may formulate it

---

[4] Cf. Gottlob Frege, *The Foundations of Arithmetic* (Oxford: Basil Blackwell, 1950), pp. 16-17; first published in 1884.

[5] "Experience cannot offer the smallest ground for the necessity of a proposition. She can observe and record what has happened; but she cannot find, in any case, or in any accumulation of cases, any reason for what *must* happen. She may see objects side by side, but she cannot see a reason why they must ever be side by side. She finds certain events to occur in succession; but the succession supplies, in its occurrence, no reasons for its recurrence; she contemplates external objects; but she cannot detect any internal bond, which indissolubly connects the future with the past, the possible with the real. To learn a proposition by experience, and to see it to be necessarily true, are two altogether different processes of thought. . . . If anyone does not clearly comprehend this distinction of necessary and contingent truths, he will not be able to go along with us in our researches into the foundations of human knowledge; nor indeed, to pursue with success any speculation on the subject." William Whewell, *Philosophy of the Inductive Sciences Founded upon Their History*, I (London: J. W. Parker & Son, 1840), 59-61.

[6] *Critique of Pure Reason*, B4; cf. *Immanuel Kant's Critique of Pure Reason*, ed. Norman Kemp Smith (London: Macmillan & Co., Ltd., 1933), p. 44.

in a sentence prefixed by the model operator "necessarily," or "it is necessary that"—then our knowledge is not a posteriori.

A priori knowledge   Here, as elsewhere, the "sceptic" and the "intuitionist" may appeal to the same fact. Affirming that ordinary empirical procedures yield no knowledge of necessary truths, the "sceptic" will conclude that there is no such knowledge and the "intuitionist," that such knowledge is intuitive. The "intuitionist's" case, for whatever it may be worth, is somewhat better here than it is in some of the other controversial areas of knowledge to which we have referred. For in some of those other areas, the "intuition" to which he wants to appeal seems simply not to be found. But in the present area, the experience to which he refers is a familiar one—whether or not that experience yields the knowledge that he thinks it does. In support of this contention only—that the experience to which the intuitionist refers is a familiar one—let us try to locate and identify the experience that he calls "intuitive." The best way to do this, I believe, is to follow the traditional account.

"Contemplation of essences," a phrase that is frequently used in this connection, is misleading, for it suggests Plato's doctrine that in order to acquire a knowledge of necessity, we should turn away from "the twilight of becoming and perishing" and contemplate the world of "the absolute and eternal and immutable." [7] According to Aristotle, however, and to subsequent philosophers in the tradition with which we are here concerned, one way of obtaining the requisite intuition is to consider the particular, perishable things of this world.

As a result of perceiving a particular blue thing, or a number of particular blue things, we may come to know what it is for a thing to be blue, and thus, we may be said to know what the property of being blue is. And as a result of perceiving a particular red thing, or a number of particular red things, we may come to know what it is for a thing to be red, and thus, to know what the property of being red is. Then, having this knowledge of what it is to be red and of what it is to be blue, we are able to see that being red excludes being blue, and that this is necessarily so.

Thus, Aristotle tells us that as a result of perceiving Callias and a number of other particular men, we come to see what it is for a thing to have the property of being human. And then, by considering the property of being human, we come to see that being human includes being animal, and that this is necessarily so.[8]

The following stages seem to be present in both of these examples: (1) the perception of the individual things—in the one case, the per-

[7] *The Republic*, 479-508.
[8] *Posterior Analytics*, 100a-100b.

ception of the particular red things and blue things, and in the other, the perception of Callias and the other particular men; (2) a process of abstraction—we come to see what it is for a thing to be red and for a thing to be blue, and we come to see what it is for a thing to be a man; (3) the intuitive apprehension of certain relations holding between properties—in the one case, apprehension of the fact that being red excludes being blue, and in the other, apprehension of the fact that being rational and animal includes being animal; and (4) this intuitive knowledge justifies a universal generalization about particular things— "Necessarily, everything is such that if it is red then it is not blue" and "Necessarily, everything is such that if it is human then it is animal."

Aristotle called this process "induction." But since it differs in essential respects from what subsequently came to be known as "induction," some other term, say, "intuitive induction," may be less misleading.[9]

If we have performed an "intuitive induction" in the manner described, then we may say that the proposition concerning the relation between properties ("Necessarily, being red excludes being blue") justifies the universal generalization about particular things ("Necessarily, everything is such that if it is red then it is not blue"). And we can say, therefore, that the universal generalization, as well as the proposition about properties, is known a priori. The order of justification thus differs from that of the enumerative induction considered earlier, where one attempts to justify the statement about properties by reference to a generalization about particular things.

There is a superficial resemblance between "intuitive induction" and "induction by simple enumeration," since in each case, we start with particular instances and then proceed beyond them. Thus, when we make an induction by enumeration, we may proceed from "This *A* is *B*," "That *A* is *B*," and so on, to "In all probability, all *A*'s are *B*'s," or to "In all probability, the next *A* is *B*." But in an induction by enumeration, the function of the particular instances is to *justify* the conclusion. If we find subsequently that our perceptions of the particular instances were unveridical, say, that the things we took to be *A*'s were not *A*'s at all, then the inductive argument would lose whatever force it may have had. In an "intuitive induction," however, the particular

---

[9] This term was proposed by W. E. Johnson, *Logic* (London: Cambridge University Press, 1921), Part II, pp. 191ff. Aristotle uses the term "induction" in the passages cited in the *Posterior Analytics*; cf. *The Nicomachean Ethics*, Book VI, Chap. 3, 1139b.

perceptions are only incidental to the conclusion. This may be seen in the following way.

Let us suppose that the knowledge expressed by the two sentences "Necessarily, being red excludes being blue" and "Necessarily, being human includes being animal" is arrived at by intuitive induction; and let us suppose further that in each case, the process began with the perception of certain particular things. Neither conclusion depends for its *justification* upon the particular perceptions which led to the knowledge concerned. As Duns Scotus put it, the perception of the particular things is only the "occasion" of acquiring the knowledge. If we happen to find our perception was unveridical, this finding will have no bearing upon the result. "If the senses from which these terms were received were all false, or what is more deceptive, if some were false and others true, I still maintain that the intellect would not be deceived about such principles. . . ." [10] If what we take to be Callias is not a man at all, but only a clever imitation of a man, then, if the imitation is clever enough, our deceptive experience will still be an occasion for contemplating the property of being human—the property of being both rational and animal—and thus, for coming to know that being human includes being animal.

It may be, indeed, that to perform an intuitive induction—i.e., to "abstract" a certain property, contemplate it, and then see what it includes and excludes—we need only to *think* of some individual thing as having that property. By thinking about a blue thing and a red thing, for example, we may come to see that being blue excludes being red. Thus, Ernst Mach spoke of "experiments in the imagination." [11] And E. Husserl, whose language may have been needlessly Platonic, said, "The Eidos, the *pure essence,* can be exemplified intuitively in the data of experience, data of perception, memory, and so forth, but just as readily *also in the mere data of fancy. . . .*" [12]

One could go on to say that "intuitive induction" enables us to know those truths about *states of affairs* which, according to the view we are trying to set forth, comprise the subject matter of logic. As a

[10] *Philosophical Writings*, ed. and trans. Allan Wolter (New York: Thomas Nelson & Sons, 1962), p. 109 (the Nelson philosophical texts); cf. p. 103. Cf. Leibniz: "It is also well to observe that if I should discover any demonstrative truth, mathematical or other, while dreaming (as might in fact be), it would be just as certain as if I had been awake. This shows us how intelligible truth is independent of the truth or of the existence outside of us of sensible and material things." *The Philosophical Works of Leibniz*, ed. G. M. Duncan (New Haven: The Tittle, Morehouse & Taylor Co., 1908), p. 161.

[11] *Erkenntnis und Irrtum* (Leipzig: Felix Meiner, 1905), p. 180ff.

[12] *Ideas: General Introduction to Phenomenology* (New York: The Macmillan Company, 1931), p. 57.

result of our perception, possibly unveridical, of some actual event, we come to consider a certain state of affairs which this event (we believe) happens to exemplify; by contemplating this state of affairs (say, the sun being in the sky and people standing in the road) we come to see that it excludes a certain other state of affairs (that disjunctive state of affairs which is either the sun not being in the sky or there being no people in the road). By contemplating this general state of affairs, we arrive at the intuitive knowledge of an even more general truth—the one that the logician might put by saying, "For any propositions *p* and *q*, the conjunction of *p* and *q* is true if, and only if, the disjunction of not-*p* and not-*q* is false."

But some of the truths of reason are said to be known "by demonstration" and not "by intuition." Thus, Locke tells us that we acquire "demonstrative knowledge" in the following situation: We have intuitive knowledge that a certain state of affairs A obtains; we also have intuitive knowledge that A includes a state of affairs B; and further, we have intuitive knowledge that B includes a state of affairs C; in which case (Locke says), whether or not we have intuitive knowledge that C obtains, we have all that is necessary in order to "demonstrate" to ourselves that C obtains. Locke reminds us, however, that proofs involving a number of steps take time, with the result that the "evident lustre" of the early steps may be lost by the time we reach the conclusion: "In long deductions, and the use of many proofs, the memory does not always so readily retain." Therefore, he said demonstrative knowledge "is more imperfect than intuitive knowledge." [13]

The various truths of reason, whether they are themselves the objects of intuitive knowledge or of demonstrative knowledge, are thus said to be at the basis of all demonstrative knowledge. We might say in more general terms: if a man knows that a certain state of affairs A necessarily obtains, and if he has intuitive or demonstrative knowledge that A includes a state of affairs B, then (provided he concludes that B obtains) he has demonstrative knowledge that B obtains.

---

[13] *Essay Concerning Human Understanding*, Book IV, Chap. 2, Sec. 7. Descartes also notes that memory is essential to demonstrative knowledge. He remarks in *Rules for the Direction of the Mind* that if we can *remember* having deduced a certain conclusion step by step from a set of premises that are "known by intuition," then, even though we may not now recall each of the particular steps, we are justified in saying that the conclusion is "known by deduction." See *The Philosophical Works of Descartes*, ed. E. S. Haldane and G. R. T. Ross, I (London: Cambridge University Press, 1934), 8. Some version of Descartes' principle should be added to the principles about memory set forth in Chap. 3. Cf. Norman Malcolm's suggestion: "If a man previously had grounds for being sure that *p*, and now remembers that *p*, but does not remember what his grounds were," then he "*has* the same grounds he previously had." *Knowledge and Certainty* (Englewood Cliffs: Prentice-Hall, Inc., 1963), p. 230.

Scepticism and "psychologism" One alternative to this metaphysical account of our knowledge of the truths of reason is scepticism: one may deny that we have such knowledge.

As we have seen, the general reply to a scepticism that addresses itself to an entire area of knowledge can only be this: we do have the knowledge in question, and therefore, any philosophical theory implying that we do not is false. This way of looking at the matter may seem especially plausible in the present instance. It is tempting to say of scepticism, with respect to the truths of reason, what Leonard Nelson said of it, with respect to the truths of mathematics. The advocate of such a scepticism, Nelson said, has invited us to "sacrifice the clearest and most lucid knowledge that we possess—indeed, the *only* knowledge that is clear and lucid *per se*. I prefer to strike the opposite course. If a philosophy, no matter how attractive or plausible or ingenious it may be, brings me into conflict with mathematics, I conclude that not mathematics but my philosophy is on the wrong track."[14] There is certainly no *better* ground for scepticism with respect to our knowledge of the truths of reason than there is for scepticism with respect to our knowledge of physical things.[15] But we should remind ourselves, at this point, of the general difficulties we encountered in trying to deal with the problem of the criterion.

The "dialectic" will proceed as before: We look for a "reductive" alternative to scepticism and intuitionism, one that will translate sentences expressing the truths in question into sentences referring to a less objectionable subject matter. Of the attempts at such reduction, the only ones worthy of consideration are, first, the view that came to be known in the nineteenth century as "psychologism," and secondly, its contemporary counterpart, which we might call "linguisticism." Much of what can be said in criticism of the one can also be said, mutatis mutandis, in criticism of the other.

Theodore Lipps wrote, in 1880, that "logic is either the physics of thought or nothing at all" and he tried to show that the truths of logic are, in fact, truths about the ways in which people think.[16] This is the

[14] Leonard Nelson, *Socratic Method and Critical Philosophy* (New Haven: Yale University Press, 1949), p. 184.

[15] "The preference of (say) seeing over understanding as a method of observation seems to me capricious. For just as an opaque body may be seen, so a concept may be understood or grasped." Alonzo Church, "Abstract Entities in Semantic Analysis," *Proceedings of the American Academy of Arts and Sciences*, Vol. 80 (1951), 100-112; the quotation is on p. 104.

[16] "*Die Aufgabe der Erkenntnistheorie,*" *Philosophische Monatshefte*, Vol. XVI, (1880); quoted by Husserl, in *Logische Untersuchungen*, Vol. I (Halle: Max Niemeyer, 1928). In his *Philosophie der Arithmetik* (Leipzig: C. E. M. Pfeffer, 1891), Husserl defended a version of "psychologism," but he criticizes that view in the *Logische Untersuchungen*.

view that was called "psychologism" and it was applied generally to the subject matter of the truths of reason.

A psychologistic interpretation of "Necessarily, being red excludes being blue" might be: "Everyone is so constituted psychologically that if he thinks of a thing as being red then he cannot help but think of it as not being blue." And a psychologistic interpretation of the logical truth "For any propositions *p* and *q*, if *p* is true and *p* implies *q*, then *q* is true" might be: "Everyone is so constituted psychologically that if he believes that *p* is true, and if he believes that *p* implies *q*, then he cannot help but believe that *q* is true."

But obviously, these psychological sentences do not at all convey what is intended by the sentences they are supposed to translate. The psychological sentences are empirical generalizations about the ways in which people think, and as such, they can be supported only by extensive psychological investigation. Thus, Gottlob Frege said, in connection with the psychologistic interpretation of mathematics: "It would be strange if the most exact of all the sciences had to seek support from psychology, which is still feeling its way none too surely." [17] And being empirical generalizations, the psychological sentences are probable at best and are at the mercy of contrary instances. The existence somewhere of one unreasonable individual—one man who believed that some things are both red and blue, or one man who believed that a certain proposition *p* is true and also that *p* implies *q*, and who yet refused to believe that *q* is true—would be sufficient to insure that the psychological sentence is false. And we know, all too well, that there are such men. Their existence, however, has no bearing upon the truths expressed by "Necessarily, being red excludes being blue" and "Necessarily, for any propositions *p* and *q*, if *p* is true and if *p* implies *q*, then *q* is true."

In the face of such difficulties, the proponent of psychologism is likely to modify his view. He will say of sentences expressing the laws of logic and the other truths of reason, that they really express *rules of thought*, and that they are not descriptive sentences telling us how

[17] *The Foundations of Arithmetic* (Oxford: Basil Blackwell, 1950), p. 38; Frege's work was first published in 1884. Cf. Philip E. B. Jourdain, *The Philosophy of Mr. B*rtr*nd R*ss*ll* (London: George Allen & Unwin, 1918), p. 88: "The psychological founding of logic appears to be not without analogy with the surprising method of advocates of evolutionary ethics, who expect to discover what *is* good by inquiring what cannibals have *thought* good. I sometimes feel inclined to apply the historical method to the multiplication table. I should make a statistical inquiry among school-children, before their pristine wisdom has been biased by teachers. I should put down their answers as to what 6 times 9 amounts to, I should work out the average of their answers to six places of decimals, and should then decide that, at the present stage of human development, this average is of the value of 6 times 9."

people actually do think. But to see the hopelessness of this approach we have only to consider the possible ways of interpreting the sentence "The laws of logic are rules of thought."

(1) One interpretation would be: "The laws of logic are ethical truths pertaining to our duties and obligations with respect to thinking." In this case, the problem of our knowledge of the laws of logic is transferred to the (more difficult) problem of our knowledge of the truths (if any) of ethics.

(2) "The laws of logic are imperatives commanding us to think in certain ways—and imperatives are neither true nor false." This way of looking at the matter leaves us with the problem of distinguishing between valid and invalid imperatives. For there is a distinction between "Do not believe, with respect to any particular thing, both that it is red and that it is blue" and "Do not believe, with respect to any particular thing, that that thing is either red or not red." The former imperative, surely, is correct or valid, and the latter, incorrect or invalid. If we are not to fall back into scepticism, we must also say that the former is known to be valid and the latter is known to be invalid. Moreover, it is not possible to construe all of the statements of logic as imperatives. For the logician can also tell us nonimperatively such things as: If you believe that p, and if you believe that p implies q, and if you conform to the imperative, modus ponens, then you will also believe that q. This statement is a necessary truth. (A manual of chess, similarly, may give us certain rules in the form of imperatives: "Move the king only one square at a time." And possibly these imperatives are neither valid nor invalid. But whether or not they are valid, the chess manual will also contain true indicative sentences—sentences which are not themselves imperatives but which tell us what will happen when, in accordance with the imperatives that the manual lays down, we move the pieces into various positions. "It is impossible, if white is in such and such a position, for black to win in less than seven moves." And these statements are also necessary truths.)

(3) "The laws of logic tell us which ways of believing will lead to truth and which will lead to falsehood." According to this interpretation, our two examples might be thought of as telling us respectively: "A necessary condition of avoiding false beliefs is to refrain from believing, with respect to any particular thing, both that that thing is red and also that it is blue" and "A necessary condition of avoiding false beliefs is to refrain from believing, at one and the same time, with respect to any propositions p and q, that p is true, that p implies q, and that q is false." To see that this way of formulating psychologism leaves us with our problem, let us compare it with a similar psychologistic interpretation of some other subject matter, say, astronomy. We may say, if we like,

that what the statement "There are nine planets" really tells us is that if we wish to avoid error with respect to the number of planets, it is essential to refrain from believing that there are not nine planets; it also tells us that if we wish to arrive at the truth about the number of planets, it is essential to believe that there *are* nine planets. It is not likely that in so spinning out what is conveyed by "There are nine planets," we can throw any light upon what the astronomer thinks he knows. In any case, our problem reappears when we compare our new versions of the statements of logic with those of the statements of astronomy. The former, but not the latter, can be prefixed by "It is necessary that," and unless we give in to scepticism (which it was the point of psychologism to avoid) we must say that the result of such a prefixing is also a statement we can know to be true.[18]

"Linguisticism"   A popular conception of the truths of reason at the present time is the linguistic analogue of psychologism. Versions of "linguisticism" may be obtained merely by altering our exposition of psychologism. We may replace the references to ways in which people *think* by references to ways in which they *use language*, replace the references to what people *believe* by references to what they *write* or *say*, replace "avoiding false belief" by "avoiding absurdity," and replace "rules of thought" by "rules of language." The result could then be criticized substantially, mutatis mutandis, as before.

Some of the versions of linguisticism, however, are less straightforward. It is often said, for example, that the sentences formulating the truths of logic are "true in virtue of the rules of language" and hence, that they are "true in virtue of the way in which we use words." What could this possibly mean?

The two English sentences, "Being red excludes being blue" and "Being rational and animal includes being animal," could plausibly be said to "owe their truth," in part, to the way in which we use words. If we used "being blue" to refer to the property of being heavy, and not to that of being blue, then the first sentence (provided the other words in it had their present use) would be false instead of true. And if we used the word "and" to express the relation of disjunction instead of conjunction, then the second sentence (again, provided that the other words in it had their present use) would also be false instead of true. But as W. V. Quine has reminded us, "even so factual a sentence as 'Brutus killed Caesar' owes its truth not only to the killing but equally

---

[18] Cf. the criticism of psychologism in Husserl's *Logische Untersuchungen*, I, 154ff., and Rudolf Carnap, *The Logical Foundations of Probability* (Chicago: University of Chicago Press, 1950), pp. 37-42.

to our using the component words as we do." [19] Had "killed," for example, been given the use that "was survived by" happens to have, then, other things being the same, "Brutus killed Caesar" would be false instead of true.

It might be suggested, therefore, that the truths of logic and other truths of reason stand in this peculiar relationship to language: they are true "solely in virtue of the rules of our language," or "solely in virtue of the ways in which we use words." But if we take the phrase "solely in virtue of" in the way in which it would naturally be taken, then the suggestion is obviously false.

To say of a sentence that it is true *solely* in virtue of the ways in which we use words, or that it is true *solely* in virtue of the rules of our language, would be to say that the only condition that needs to obtain in order for the sentence to be true is that we use words in certain ways or that there be certain rules pertaining to the way in which words are to be used. But let us consider what conditions must obtain if the English sentence "Being red excludes being blue" is to be true. One such condition is indicated by the following sentence which we may call "*T*":

> The English sentence "Being blue excludes being red" is true if, and only if, being blue excludes being red.

Clearly, the final part of *T*, the part following the second "if," formulates a necessary condition for the truth of the English sentence "Being red excludes being blue"; but it refers to a relationship among properties and not to rules of language or ways in which we use words (To suppose otherwise would be to make the mistake, once again, of confusing use and mention of language). Hence, we cannot say that the only conditions that need to obtain in order for "Being red excludes being blue" to be true is that we use words in certain ways or that there be certain rules pertaining to the ways in which words are to be used; and therefore, the sentence cannot be said to be true solely in virtue of the ways in which we use words.

Logical truth and the analytic   Another epistemological problem involving the truths of reason concerns the status of "the synthetic a priori." To understand this problem, we must first explicate the terms involved.

Let us consider, once again, the epistemological terms "a priori" and "a posteriori." What they are intended to refer to may be conveyed in this way: We have said that those necessary truths that are known by "intuitive induction" or "by demonstration," in the manner set forth

---

[19] W. V. Quine, "Carnap and Logical Truth," *The Philosophy of Rudolf Carnap*, ed. P. A. Schilpp (La Salle, Ill.: Open Court Publishing Co., 1963), p. 386.

above, are truths that are known a priori. Let us also say that those universal generalizations that are justified by reference to such truths are known a priori; hence, both "Being red excludes being blue" and "Every individual thing is such that if it is red then it is not blue" will be statements expressing what we know a priori. And let us say that what is known, but not known a priori, is known a posteriori. Thus, we can say, with Kant, that *necessity* is a mark or criterion of the a priori.

The terms "analytic" and "synthetic" were introduced by Kant in order to contrast two types of categorical judgment. They are used in much of contemporary philosophy to refer instead to the types of *sentence* that express the types of judgment to which Kant referred. An analytic *judgment*, according to Kant, is a judgment in which "the predicate adds nothing to the concept of the subject." If I judge that all squares are rectangles, then, in Kant's terminology, the concept of the subject of my judgment is the property of being square, and the concept of the predicate is the property of being rectangular. Kant uses the term "analytic," since, he says, the concept of the predicate helps to "break up the concept of the subject into those constituent concepts that have all along been thought in it." [20] Since being square is the conjunctive property of being equilateral and rectangular, the predicate of the judgment expressed by "All squares are rectangular" may be said to "analyze out" what is contained in the subject. An analytic judgment, then, may be expressed in the form of an explicit redundancy: e.g., "Everything is such that if it is both equilateral and rectangular then it is rectangular." To deny such an explicit redundancy would be to affirm a contradictio in adjecto, for it would be to judge that there are things which both have and do not have a certain property—in the present instance, that there is something that both is and is not rectangular. Hence, Kant said that "the common principle of all analytic judgments is the law of contradiction." [21]

If we wish to apply Kant's distinction to *sentences*, as distinguished from *judgments*, and if we are to be otherwise faithful to what it was that he had in mind, we might proceed in the following way.

Consider a sentence that can be expressed in the form "All things that are S are P"; or more exactly, consider a sentence such that what it expresses can also be expressed in an English sentence of the form "All things that are S are P." One example of such a sentence is, "All things that are square are rectangular"; another is, "No bachelors are married," for what this sentence expresses may also be expressed obversely by, "All things that are bachelors are nonmarried." Let us say of such a sentence

[20] *Critique of Pure Reason*, A7; trans. Norman Kemp Smith.
[21] *Prolegomena to Any Future Metaphysics*, Sec. 2.

that it is *analytic* provided that the predicate term P (i.e., the term occupying the place of "P") can be "analyzed out" of the subject term S. And let us say that the predicate term P can be *analyzed out* of the subject term S provided that any one of the following three conditions holds.

(1) The terms S and P are synonymous (are used with the same meaning).

(2) S is synonymous with a conjunctive term, S^1 *and* S^2, which is such that S^2 is synonymous with P, and S^1 is not synonymous with S.

(3) P is synonymous with a disjunctive term, P^1 *or* P^2, which is such that P^1 can be analyzed out of S, and P^2 cannot be analyzed out of S.

Thus, if we use "equilateral and rectangular" as a synonym for "square," we may say that in virtue of (1), the sentence "All things that are equilateral and rectangular are square," as well as "All things that are square are square," and "All things that are equilateral and rectangular are equilateral and rectangular," is analytic. We may say that in virtue of (2), the sentence "All things that are equilateral and rectangular are rectangular" is analytic. And if we use "parents" as a synonym for "fathers or mothers," then we may say that in virtue of (3), the sentence "All fathers are parents" is analytic.

Completing this Kant-like account, we could now say that a categorical sentence—a sentence expressible in the form "All things that are S are P," "No things that are S are P," "Some things that are S are P," and "Some things that are S are not P"—is *synthetic* provided that neither it nor its negation is analytic. (Kant did not himself provide a term for the negations of analytic judgments—those judgments expressible in such sentences as "Some squares are not rectangles" and "Some bachelors are married." We could say, however, that the sentences expressing such judgments are "analytically false"—in which case we would have a motive for replacing Kant's "analytic" by "analytically true.")

If we thus restrict "analytic" and "synthetic" to categorical sentences, then we should distinguish the concept of the *analytic* from the wider, but closely related, concept of *logical truth*. It is sometimes said that a sentence is logically true if it is true "in virtue of its form alone." It would be very difficult to define this phrase precisely, but what it intends may be suggested by the following procedure, set forth by W. V. Quine.

Quine enumerates a list of expressions that he calls "logical expressions"; the list includes "and," "or," "not," "all," "every," "some," "if," "then," "it is true that," and "it is false that." He then proposes that a sentence may be called logically true provided it is one in which only the logical expressions *occur essentially*. In "If no Greeks are Romans then it is false that some Romans are Greeks," the logical expressions "no," "it is false that," "some," "if," and "then" occur essentially, but the nonlogical expressions, "are," "Greeks," and "Romans," do not. One might say that the truth of the sentence is independent of the nonlogical expressions that occur in it. Or more exactly, the sentence is one such that, if, for any nonlogical expression in the sentence, we replace each of its occurrences by any other "grammatically admissable" expression (making sure that all occurrences of the old word are replaced by occurrences of the same new word), the result will be true. Thus, if we replace "Greeks" by "Algerians," and "Romans" by "Alaskans," the result will be true; this would also hold true for any other plural nouns we might select. But if we replace some of the logical expressions by other logical expressions (e.g., "no" by "some") we may get a falsehood. A logical truth, according to this interpretation, is a sentence "which is true and remains true under all reinterpretations of its components other than logical particles." [22] Or we could say, somewhat more broadly, that a logical truth is any sentence which is such that what is expressed can also be expressed in a sentence of the sort that Quine describes.

The class of logical truths, then, is not restricted to sentences that are categorical; hence, it is wider than the class of sentences we have described as being "analytic." But all analytic sentences may be said to be logically true. Thus, again, if we use "square" as a synonym for "equilateral and rectangular," we may express "All things that are square are rectangular" as "All things that are equilateral and rectangular are rectangular"; the latter sentence could be said to be logically true, or "true in virtue of its form," since replacement of "equilateral" by any other adjective, and of each occurrence of "rectangular" by any other adjective (the same adjective each time), will result in a sentence that is also true.

We may thus divide meaningful indicative sentences into three groups: (1) those sentences that are *logically true*—analytic sentences comprise a subclass of sentences that are logically true; (2) the negations or contradictories of sentences that are logically true—these, we may say, are *logically false*; (3) and finally, all other meaningful indicative sentences—these, some of which are true and some of which are false, may be said to be *synthetic*, in a broad sense of the term "synthetic." (Using "synthetic" in this broad sense, we depart somewhat from the Kantian tradition.)

But many philosophers now believe that the distinction between

[22] Cf. W. V. Quine, *From a Logical Point of View* (Cambridge: Harvard University Press, 1953), pp. 22-23.

the analytic and the synthetic has been shown to be untenable; we should consider what reasons there might be for such a belief. Ordinarily, it is defended by reference to the following facts. (1) In drawing a distinction between analytic and synthetic sentences, one must use such a term as "synonym"; we have said, for example, that "both equilateral and rectangular" may be used as a synonym for "square." (2) The traditional account of synonymy refers to abstract entities; one term is said to be used synonymously with another term if the two terms are used to connote the same properties. (3) There is no reliable way of telling, merely by observing a man's behavior, what properties, if any, he is using any given word to connote. And (4) it is not possible to define "synonym" merely by reference to linguistic behavior.[23]

But these four propositions, all of them true, are not sufficient to yield the conclusion (5) that the distinction between the analytic and the synthetic is untenable. If we attempt to formulate the additional premise that would be needed to make the argument valid, we will see that it must involve a philosophical generalization—a generalization concerning what conditions must obtain if the distinction between the analytic and the synthetic is to be tenable. And how would the generalization be defended? This question should be considered in the light of what we have said about scepticism and the problem of the criterion. Of the philosophical generalizations that would make the above argument valid, none of them, so far as I know, has ever been defended. It is not accurate, therefore, to say that the distinction between the analytic and the synthetic has been *shown* to be untenable.

The synthetic   Some of the things that we know a priori are expressible in sen-
a priori   tences that are logically true. Presumably, all of the logical truths
cited up to now are necessary truths that are shown to be true a priori. Some of the things that we know a posteriori are expressible in sentences that are synthetic, e.g., "There are kangaroos in New Zealand." It may be that some of the things that we know a posteriori are expressible in sentences that are logically true. (A possible example of such an a posteriori logical truth would be a logical theorem which a man accepts on the ground that all reputable logicians and computing machines assert that it is true.) The question of the synthetic a priori now becomes: Of the things that we know a priori to be true, are any of them expressible in sentences that are synthetic? Or more briefly: Is there a synthetic a priori?

[23] Cf. W. V. Quine, "Two Dogmas of Empiricism," in *From a Logical Point of View*, esp. pp. 20-37, and Morton White, "The Analytic and the Synthetic: An Untenable Dualism," in Leonard Linsky, ed. *Semantics and the Philosophy of Language* (Urbana: University of Illinois Press, 1952), pp. 272-86.

Obviously, it would be very difficult indeed to *prove* either that there is a synthetic a priori or that there is not. But there are sentences which seem to express what is known a priori, and which, up to now, have not been shown to be logically true. This fact may be *some* presumption in favor of the view that there is a synthetic a priori. And if there is a synthetic a priori, then this fact, in turn, might be taken to have important bearing upon the nature of the human mind (it would imply, for example, that our a priori knowledge is not restricted to knowledge of "formal" truths).

Let us consider, then, certain possible examples of the synthetic a priori.

(1) One important candidate for the synthetic a priori is the knowledge that might be expressed either by saying "Being red includes being colored" or "Necessarily, everything that is red is colored." The sentence "Everything that is red is colored" recalls our paradigmatic "Everything that is square is rectangular." In the case of the latter sentence, we were able to "analyze the predicate out of the subject": We replaced the subject term "square" wth a conjunctive term, "equilateral and rectangular," such that one of its conjuncts is synonymous with the predicate term and the other conjunct is not synonymous with the original subject term. But it would seem to be impossible to find— or even to coin—any conjunctive term which is synonymous with "red" and which is such that one of its two conjuncts is synonymous with "colored" and the other is not synonymous with "red." It is recommended that the reader try to find, or to coin, such a term.

We may be tempted, then, to follow the procedure we took in the case of "All fathers are parents," where, it will be recalled, we replaced the predicate term "parents" by a synonymous disjunctive term, "fathers or mothers," which was such that one of its disjuncts, being synonymous with the subject term "fathers," could be "analyzed out" of the subject. Thus, we might hope to replace the predicate term of "Everything that is red is colored" by a lengthy disjunctive predicate, having for its disjuncts names of each of the colors. In this case, our new sentence might read as follows: "Everything that is red is either red or blue or green or yellow or. . . ." But we will not have replaced the original predicate "colored" by a synonym until we have removed the dots and completed the disjunction. Can we do this? Can we provide a list of colors and say truly, "These colors, red and blue and green and yellow and . . . , are all the colors there are"? And what is even more to the point, if we *can* do this, can we then go on to say that a disjunction of color words, made up from this list of colors, will constitute a *synonym* for "colored"? It would seem not, since one may say without contradiction: "It is possible that a thing may be colored and yet neither red nor blue nor green nor yellow nor. . . . There may be colors that are unknown to us—colors that we would experience if we had a rather different type of sensory apparatus." If such a suggestion is significant and consistent, as it seems to be, then "colored" is not synonymous with any expression that can be formed merely by listing each of the colors. And if this is so, then our lengthy disjunctive predicate will not be one that we have "analyzed out" of the subject, and therefore, we will not have shown that the a priori sentence "Everything that is red is colored," is analytic.[24]

It has been suggested that the sentences giving rise to the problem of the synthetic a priori are really "postulates about the meanings of words," and therefore, that they do not express what is synthetic a priori. But if the suggestion is intended literally, then it would seem to betray the confusion between use and mention that we encountered earlier. A postulate about the meaning of the word "red," for example, or a sentence expressing such a postulate, would presumably mention the word "red." It might read, "The word 'red' may be taken to refer to a certain color," or perhaps, "Let the word 'red' be taken to refer to a certain color." But "Everything that is red is colored," although it uses the words "red" and "colored," doesn't mention them at all. Thus, there would seem to be no clear sense in which it could be said really to be a "meaning postulate" or to refer in any way to words and how they are used.

(2) What Leibniz called the "disparates" furnish us with a second candidate for the synthetic a priori. These are closely related to the type of sentence just considered, but involve problems that are essentially different. An example of a sentence concerned with disparates would be our earlier "Being red excludes being blue" or (alternatively put) "Necessarily, nothing that is red is blue." [25] Philosophers have devoted considerable ingenuity to trying to show that "Nothing that is red is blue" can be expressed as a sentence that is analytic, and thus, as a logical truth, but so far as I have been able to determine, all of these attempts have been unsuccessful. Again, it is recommended that the reader try for himself to re-express "Nothing that is red is blue" in such a way that the predicate may be "analyzed out" of the subject in any of the senses described above.

(3) It has also been held, not without plausibility, that certain ethical sentences express what is synthetic a priori. Thus, Leibniz, writ-

---

[24] Cf. C. H. Langford, "A Proof that Synthetic A Priori Propositions Exist," *Journal of Philosophy*, XLVI (1949), 20-24.

[25] Cf. John Locke, *Essay Concerning Human Understanding*, Book IV, Chap. 1, Sec. 7; G. W. Leibniz, *New Essays Concerning Human Understanding*, Book IV, Chap. 2, Sec. 1; Franz Brentano, *Versuch über die Erkenntnis* (Leipzig: Felix Meiner, 1925), pp. 9-10.

ing on what he called the "supersensible element" in knowledge, said: ". . . But to return to *necessary truths*, it is generally true that we know them only by this natural light, and not at all by the experience of the senses. For the senses can very well make known, in some sort, what is, but they cannot make known what *ought to be* or what could not be otherwise." [26] Or consider the sentence "Pleasure as such is intrinsically good, or good in itself, whenever and wherever it may occur." If this sentence expresses something that is known to be true, then what it expresses must be synthetic a priori. To avoid this conclusion, some philosophers deny that sentences about what is intrinsically good, or good in itself, can be known to be true.[27] An examination of this view would involve us, once again, in the problem of the criterion.

And still other things that we know a priori to be true seem to be expressible only in sentences that are synthetic.

[26] Quoted from *The Philosophical Works of Leibniz*, p. 162.
[27] Cf. the discussion of this question in chaps. 5 and 6 in William Frankena, *Ethics*, Prentice-Hall Foundations of Philosophy Series.

THE STATUS

OF APPEARANCES

6

The problem   When a man sees an external thing, say, a tree, his perception
of   is the result of a complex physiological and psychological process.
Democritus   Light reflected from the thing stimulates the rod cells and cone
cells in his eyes; in consequence of this stimulation, there is a further effect within the brain which, in turn, produces a visual sensation.
Perception by means of the other sense organs is similar. In each case,
the sensation (also referred to as the "sense impression," "appearance,"
"idea," or "sense datum") would seem to depend for its existence upon
the state of the perceiving subject. Or to proceed somewhat more cau-
tiously, the ways in which the things that we perceive *appear* to us when
we perceive them depend in part upon our own psychological and
physiological condition. This fact has led to some of the most puzzling
questions of the theory of knowledge.

Democritus took it to imply not only that we do not perceive what
it is that we think we perceive, but also that external things are not at
all what we tend to believe that they are. The appearances of things,
he said, "change with the condition of our body and the influences
coming toward it or resisting it." [1] The question as to whether any
particular thing will appear white, black, yellow, red, sweet, or bitter,
he noted, cannot be answered merely by reference to the nature of
the thing; one must also refer to the nature of the person or animal
who is perceiving the thing. And from these premises, which are un-
deniable, Democritus then went on to infer (1) that no one ever
perceives any external thing to be white, black, yellow, red, sweet, or
bitter, and also (2), that no unperceived external thing *is*, in fact, white,
black, yellow, red, sweet, or bitter.

[1] Fragment quoted from Milton Nahm, *Selections from Early Greek Philosophy*
(New York: Appleton-Century-Crofts, 1934), p. 209; cf. pp. 173-87, 194-95.

91

The same premises have also been used to support other, equally extreme, conclusions. Oversimplifying slightly, we may say that Democritus reasoned in this way: "The wine that tastes sweet to me tastes sour to you; therefore, I do not perceive that it is sweet and you do not perceive that it is sour, and the wine itself is neither sweet nor sour." Protagoras, however, reasoned in a somewhat different way: "The wine that tastes sweet to me tastes sour to you; hence, I perceive that it is sweet and you perceive that it is sour; and therefore, one cannot say absolutely either that the wine is sweet or that the wine is sour; one can only say relativistically that whereas it is true for me that the wine is sweet, it is true for you that the wine is sour." [2] And some of the American New Realists, in defense of the view that "things *are* just what they *seem*," drew still another conclusion: "The wine that tastes sweet to me tastes sour to you; therefore, one must say (absolutely and not relativistically) that there are contradictions in nature; one must say of the wine not only that it is both sweet and not sweet, but also that it is both sour and not sour." [3]

Variants of these arguments may be found not only in writings on popular science ("Physics and psychology teach us that the world is not at all like what we perceive"), but also in the works of distinguished psychologists and philosophers. Some philosophers, in order to avoid such extreme conclusions, have been led to question the premises. It has been suggested, for example, that the appearances of things may only *appear* to change with the condition of our body.[4] It has also been suggested that things may not actually appear in different ways—that it is a mistake to suppose that by altering either our perceptual apparatus or the conditions of observation, we can produce anything that might properly be called a change in the way in which a physical thing appears.[5] But such extreme measures are not at all necessary. We can accept the premises that Democritus used and, at the same time, reject his conclusions, for the conclusions do not follow from the premises. This would also hold true for the other versions of the argument.

[2] See the discussion of Protagoras' view in Plato's *Theaetetus*, p. 145.

[3] Cf. E. B. Holt, Ralph Barton Perry, and others, *The New Realism* (New York: The Macmillan Company, 1912), pp. 2, 365. For a more detailed discussion of New Realism and the views to which it led, see Roderick M. Chisholm, *Realism and the Background of Phenomenology* (New York: Free Press of Glencoe, Inc., 1960), and Roderick M. Chisholm, "Theory of Knowledge," in *Philosophy* (Englewood Cliffs: Prentice-Hall, Inc., 1964; Humanistic Scholarship in America, The Princeton Studies), by Roderick M. Chisholm, Herbert Feigl, William K. Frankena, John Passmore, and Manley Thompson.

[4] Cf. G. E. Moore, *Philosophical Studies* (London: Routledge & Kegan Paul, Ltd., 1922), p. 245.

[5] This suggestion seems to be presupposed by passages in J. L. Austin's *Sense and Sensibilia* (New York: Oxford University Press, Inc., 1962). Cf. the criticism of this book in Roderick Firth's "Austin and the Argument from Illusion," *Philosophical Review*, LXXIII (1964), 372-82.

Referring to Democritus, Aristotle wrote: "The earlier students of nature were mistaken in their view that without sight there was no white or black, without taste no savour. This statement of theirs is partly true, partly false. 'Sense' and 'the sensible object' are ambiguous terms; i.e., they may denote either potentialities or actualities. The statement is true of the latter, false of the former. This ambiguity they wholly failed to notice." [6]

In suggesting that the terms "white" and "black" are ambiguous, Aristotle is taking note of the fact that in certain uses, these terms are intended to refer to ways of appearing and that in other uses they are intended to refer to certain properties or dispositions of physical things —those properties or dispositions in virtue of which the things appear in the ways in which they do appear. If a physical thing *is* white, if it has the properties or dispositions to which Aristotle referred, then it is such that, when it is viewed by an ordinary observer under favorable lighting conditions, it will appear white to that observer. The physicist can tell us in detail just what the conditions are that a thing must satisfy if it is to have this property; that is to say, he can tell us just what characteristics a physical surface must have if it is to appear white to a normal observer in ordinary light. Let us say of such terms as "white," "black," "yellow," "red," "bitter," and "sweet," that when they are used to refer to these properties or dispositions, they have a *dispositional* use, and that when they are used to refer to ways of appearing, to ways in which things may appear, they have a *sensible* use. Aristotle is telling us, then, that the statement "Without sight, there is no white or black, without taste, no savour" is true if the terms "white," "black," and "savour" have a sensible use, and false if they have a dispositional use. Democritus, therefore, seems to have committed the fallacy of equivocation: Having established that the statement is true when it is taken in the first of these two ways, he goes on to infer fallaciously that it is also true when it is taken in the second.

And it is clear that in the passages referred to, Democritus does not establish his thesis about perception—his thesis that no one ever *perceives* any object to be white, black, yellow, red, bitter, or sweet. For the only argument that he presents in favor of this thesis is the fallacious argument in favor of his thesis concerning the nature of physical things.

Similar objections apply to the other versions of the argument. In each of the three versions considered, the terms "sweet" and "sour" have their sensible use in the premise ("The wine that tastes sweet to me tastes sour to you") and their dispositional use in the conclusion.

[6] *De Anima,* Book III, Chap. 2, p. 426a; see also *Metaphysics,* Book IV, Chap. 5, 1010b.

The deceptive character of all three versions of the argument might be said to lie in the fact that certain truths about appearances are mistaken for truths about the things that present those appearances. From the fact that a thing's *appearing* white depends upon the condition of the perceiver, one infers mistakenly that the thing's *being* white is also something that depends upon the condition of the perceiver.

It is also possible to err in the other direction. One may make the mistake of supposing, with respect to certain truths about the things that appear to us, that they are also truths that hold of the appearances that those things present.

One such mistake, very frequently made, is that of supposing that if we perceive a physical thing, then we also *perceive* its appearances— that we see its visual appearances, hear its auditory appearances, feel its tactual appearances. But this is to misconceive the nature of perception. We perceive a thing when the thing as stimulus object has acted upon our sense organs, thereby causing us to be appeared to. The appearances of things, however, are not stimulus objects that affect our sense organs and therefore they are not themselves anything that we perceive. We do not see, hear, or feel the appearances of things.

Another such mistake may be more pernicious. From the fact that a physical thing *appears* white, for example, one might infer mistakenly that the thing presents an appearance which *is* white, and hence, that there are certain physical things and certain appearances which are alike in color. If this inference were sound, one could also say that, under favorable conditions of observation, the appearances of things have the same color as do the things themselves, in which case appearances could be said to *resemble* their objects in important respects. Thus, Lucretius suggested that when a man perceives a tree, a *simulacrum*— a small physical object having the characteristics that the tree is seen to have—is produced inside the head.[7] Subsequent philosophers have said that the appearance may "picture" or even "duplicate" the thing that appears.[8] And why *not* say that if a physical thing appears white, then it presents an appearance which *is* white?

For one thing, it is clear that the inference from "Something appears *F*" to "Something presents an appearance that *is F*" is not in

[7] *On the Nature of Things,* Book IV.

[8] "No man doubts that when he brings to mind the look of a dog he owned when a boy, there is something of a canine sort immediately present to and therefore compresent with his consciousness, but that it is quite certainly not that dog in the flesh." A. O. Lovejoy, *The Revolt against Dualism* (New York: W. W. Norton & Company, Inc., 1930), p. 305. This view has been called "the representative theory of perception." But it would seem advisable to avoid such expressions (along with "realism," "direct realism," "indirect realism," "critical realism," and the like), since they have come to be used in many different and conflicting ways by people who write about philosophy.

general valid. For there are adjectives which are such that, if we replace "*F*" by any of those adjectives, then "Something appears *F*" will be true and "Something presents an appearance which is *F*" will be false. From "The man appears tubercular," we may not infer "The man presents an appearance which is tubercular," and from "The books appear worn and dusty and more than two hundred years old," we may not infer "The books present appearances which are worn and dusty and more than two hundred years old."

Moreover, there is an absurdity inherent in saying that an appearance and a physical thing may have the same color. If we say of a physical thing that it is white, we are saying that the thing is such that, when it is viewed by a normal observer under favorable conditions, then it will appear white. Suppose, then, that "It will appear white" does imply "It will present an appearance which is white," where "is white" has the sense that it has when it is applied to a physical thing. In such a case, a white, physical thing would be something such that, when it is viewed by a normal observer under favorable conditions, it will present an appearance which is such that, when *it*—the appearance—is viewed under favorable conditions, then it will present a (second-order) appearance which is white; the (second-order) appearance will therefore be such that, when it is viewed under favorable conditions, then it will present a (third-order) appearance which is such that . . . and so on, *ad indefinitum.*

If we thus assimilate appearances to substances or concrete things, we multiply entities—and problems—beyond necessity. We find ourselves confronted, for example, with such strange questions as: If the appearance can be white in the sense in which a rose can be white, does it also have a certain weight, an inside, and a backside? Could it be that the backside of the white appearance, the side that (somehow) faces away, is green, or blue, or yellow?

But what is the appearance if it is not a substance or concrete thing?

The adverbial theory   When we say "The appearance of the thing is white," our language suggests that we are attributing a certain property to a substance. But we could just as well have said "The thing appears white," using the verb "appears" instead of the substantive "appearance." And in "The thing appears white," as already noted, the word "white" functions as an adverb.[9] Ordinarily, the point of an adverb is not to

---

[9] The point is developed in detail by C. J. Ducasse, *Nature, Mind and Death* (La Salle, Ill.: Open Court Publishing Co., 1949), Chap. 13. This general view of appearing is suggested by Thomas Reid, in his *Essays on the Intellectual Powers of Man*, Essay I, Chap. 1, Sec. 12, and by G. F. Stout, in "Are Presentations Mental or Physical?" *Proceedings of the Aristotelian Society*, n.s., Vol. IX (1909).

attribute a property to a substance, but to attribute a property to another property ("He is exceptionally tall") or to attribute a property to an event, process, or state of affairs ("He is walking slowly"). We might say, then, that the word "white," in what we have called its sensible use, tells us something about that state of affairs which is an object's appearing; it tells us something about the *way* in which the object appears, just as "slowly" may tell us something about the way in which an object moves.

We have noted, however, that a man may be presented with a "white appearance" when no object is appearing (say, when he is thinking about a possible white object). Hence, if we are to speak more strictly, we should not say that "white," in its sensible use, always refers to the way in which an object appears; it refers, rather, to the way in which one is *appeared to*—whether or not an object appears. Or if we introduce an active verb such as "sensing" or "experiencing" as a synonym for the passive "is appeared to," we could say that "white," in its sensible use, refers to the way in which a man may sense or experience.

No longer needing such expressions as "white appearance," we need not countenance the question as to whether the white appearance has a certain weight, or a backside, or an inside. And thus, we need not wonder whether the backside of a white appearance might be green, or blue, or yellow. We need not ask whether appearances might exist unsensed—whether, in Bertrand Russell's terms, there are "unsensed sensibilia." [10] And we need not ask whether appearances might be identical with parts of the external physical things that we perceive—whether the white appearance that we sense might be identical with the surface of the white object that we see. For in saying "He is appeared to white," or "He senses whitely," we are not committed to saying that there *is* a thing—an appearance—of which the word "white," in its sensible use, designates a property. We are saying, rather, that there is a certain state or process—that of being appeared to, or sensing, or experiencing—and we are using the adjective "white," or the adverb "whitely," to describe more specifically the way in which that process occurs.

The phenomenological problem   One may feel, however, that this "adverbial" theory leaves something out. Even if the appearance is not a *simulacrum* of the object that appears, the relation between the appearance and the object may seem to be more intimate than the "adverbial" theory, as we have it so far, would allow. The problem of saying just what this relationship is may be called the phenomenological problem of appear-

[10] See the essay "The Relation of Sense-Data to Physics," in Russell's *Mysticism and Logic* (New York: W. W. Norton & Company, Inc., 1929); this book was first published in 1918.

ances. The facts are familiar to everyone, but it is difficult to describe them without either overestimating or underestimating the role of appearances and without drawing unwarranted philosophical conclusions. The principal facts, I believe, are four.

(1) We perceive the object to have the characteristics we do perceive it to have, partly *because* of the way in which it appears to us. If the objects that we now perceive happened to appear in certain ways *other* than those in which they are now appearing, then we would not be perceiving them to be the objects that we are now perceiving them to be. It does not follow from these facts, however, that to perceive something to be, say, a tree, is to "make a causal inference" or "to frame the hypothesis" that a tree is one of the causes of the way in which one is being appeared to. Perceiving no more consists in deducing the causes of appearing, than reading consists in deducing the causes of ink marks.

(2) As we emphasized earlier, the appearance of a physical object —the way of being appeared to which the object as stimulus serves to cause—plays a fundamental role in the context of *justification*. If I ask myself Socratically what my justification is for thinking that it is a *tree* that I see, and if I continue my self-examination in the way we attempted to describe in Chapter 2, I will reach a point at which I will justify my claim about the tree by appeal to a proposition about the way in which I am appeared to.

(3) A point of a rather different sort follows from one of the familiar features of perception. Whenever we *see* a physical object, then we also see certain parts of that object and fail to see certain other parts of that object. (But from the fact that we fail to perceive certain parts of the object, it does not follow that we fail to perceive the object. Verbs of perception are like "to be located in" and unlike "to contain." If one object contains another, then it contains every part of the other; hence, New Hampshire contains every part of Jaffrey. But one object may be located in another without being located in every part of the other; what is in New Hampshire need not also be in Jaffrey.[11]) As the use of a microscope may suggest, every part that we see has parts of its own that we do not see. Similar remarks apply to perception by means of any of the other senses: Whenever we perceive an object by means of any one of the senses, there are certain parts of that object that we perceive and certain other parts of it that we do not perceive. With refer-

---

[11] C. D. Broad once argued that, inasmuch as we do not see every part of the bell on any of those occasions on which, as we like to think, we see a bell, therefore, strictly speaking, we never see a bell at all; see his *Mind and Its Place in Nature* (New York: Harcourt, Brace & World, Inc., 1925), pp. 149-50. This is like saying that, since the butcher doesn't cut every part of the roast, therefore, strictly speaking, he doesn't cut the roast at all.

ence to these facts, we may now make our third point concerning the relation between perceiving and being appeared to: Whenever we perceive an object, then the object appears to us in a certain way; each of the parts that we perceive also appears to us in a certain way; and those parts that we do not perceive do not appear to us in any way.

(4) Using, for the moment, the terminology of "appearances," we may also say that the appearances of the parts of the object are included in the appearances of the whole. If, for example, a man is looking at a hen, then we may say of the hen itself, and of those parts of the hen that the man happens to see, that each of these objects presents an appearance. We can say of the hen that it is a whole in which these various parts (among others) are contained; we can also say of the appearance of the hen, that it, too, is a whole in which the appearances of the various parts are contained. Indeed we might say of the appearance of each part, that it is a part of the appearance of the whole. The appearance of the outer part of the tip of one of the feathers is a part of the appearance of the feather; the appearance of the feather is a part of the appearance of the wing; the appearance of the wing is a part of the appearance of the side of the hen; and the appearance of the side of the hen is a part of the appearance of the hen. And these facts, it must be conceded, are difficult to formulate, either in the terminology of "appearing" or in the terminology of "sensing" or "being appeared to."

If we use the terminology of "appearing," we might express the facts in question as follows: "The way in which a thing appears to a man includes ways in which some, but not all, of its parts appear, and the way in which any part of a thing appears is included in the way in which the whole appears." If we use the terminology of "being appeared to," we might say: "The way in which a man is appeared to by a thing includes ways in which he is appeared to by some, but not all, of the parts of the thing, and the way in which he is appeared to by any part of the thing is included in the way in which he is appeared to by the thing." And if we use the terminology of "sensing," then we shall have to replace the "by" by some other preposition or phrase—possibly, "with respect to"—and say: "The way in which a man senses with respect to a thing includes ways in which he senses with respect to some, but not all, of the parts of the thing, and the way in which he senses with respect to any part of the thing is included in the way in which he senses with respect to the thing." It is clear that the terminology of "appearances," whatever its theoretical limitations, has a practical advantage at this point. But if I am not mistaken, the facts of the matter can be put in the terminology of "being appeared to."

Appearances and brain processes

According to what is sometimes called the "identity theory," appearances may be identified with something that is to be found in the brain, and therefore, they may be subsumed under the category of what is material or physical. The theory is defended on the ground (1) that there is known to be least a close correlation between appearances and what is cerebral or neurological, and (2) that in order not to multiply entities beyond necessity it is reasonable to suppose that a strict identity is involved rather than a mere correlation between entities that are distinct. (Prehistoric astronomers, noting the close correlations obtaining between the wanderings of the evening star and those of the morning star, may have reasoned similarly in behalf of the thesis that the evening star and the morning star are one and the same.) It is commonly believed that if the identity theory could be shown to be true, then, so far as what we know about appearances is concerned, there would be no need to assume the existence of any entities other than physical bodies and their properties, states, and processes; what we know about appearances could be accommodated to the assumption that there is "nothing in the world but increasingly complex arrangements of physical constituents." [12]

To evaluate the identity theory and the claims that have been made in its behalf, we must first decide just what it is that is being identified with what.

If we were to reject the "adverbial theory" of appearing, or being appeared to, and were to accept a substantival theory of *appearances* in its place, then our formulation of the identity theory could be reasonably straightforward. Taken substantivally, the sentence "Jones experiences a red appearance" could be said to be like "Jones eats a red tomato" in that it describes an intimate relation between Jones and a certain other substance. We could thus formulate the identity theory by saying that appearances are *parts* of the brain—chunks of grey matter, say, or cells, or strips of nervous tissue. And this is what Thomas Case, a nineteenth century advocate of "physical realism," seems to have said.

According to Case, appearances are to be identified with "physical parts of the nervous system, tactile, optic, auditory, etc., sensibly affected in various manners." Assuming that people *perceive* appearances, he was then able to say that they perceive the insides of their own bodies, not external, physical things. "The hot felt is the tactile nerves heated, the white seen is the optic nerves so coloured." He then argued that on the basis of what people perceive about their nervous systems, they make

[12] J. J. C. Smart, "Sensations and Brain Processes," in *The Philosophy of Mind*, ed. V. C. Chappell (Englewood Cliffs: Prentice-Hall, Inc., 1962), p. 161.

inferences and hypotheses about what goes on outside: "From the hot within we infer a fire without." [13]

Case thus seems to have committed the "sense-datum fallacy"; for he assumes that when the "fire without" appears hot, then there is an appearance "within" which actually has the property that the fire appears to have. He does not distinguish the sensible and dispositional uses of property words. He assumes that people perceive appearances and not external physical things. And he assumes that the process we ordinarily call perceiving, is really just a matter of framing hypotheses and making inferences, and thus he is able to conclude that we come to know external things by first examining the insides of our heads. His "physical realism," therefore, was easily parodied. (F. H. Bradley remarked that according to Case's theory, when he was offended by an unpleasant smell, what he was really aware of was "the stinking state of my own nervous system." [14])

But the identity theory need not involve the various errors that have been attributed to Case. Contemporary versions of it are considerably more difficult to criticize.

J. J. C. Smart has suggested that appearances "are nothing over and above brain processes." [15] His view thus presupposes an adverbial theory of appearing rather than a substantival theory of appearances; he is concerned with the *process* of appearing and not with certain *substances* called "appearances." Given his view, such sentences as "Jones experiences a red appearance" are misleading, for "appearance" should be replaced by "appearing." But if we are to avoid multiplying entities beyond necessity, we will not say "Jones experiences a red *appearing.*" For "Jones experiences a red appearing" suggests that there are *two* processes—one, the *experiencing,* the other, the *appearing.* We may suppose that the experiencing and the appearing—or rather, the experiencing and the being appeared to—are one and the same. Hence, we could make use of a locution similar to our earlier "Jones is appeared red to." But since we do not want to say that the word "red," in application to a *process,* has the same meaning that it has in application to a concrete thing or substance, our locution will be even less misleading if we express it, once again, as "Jones is appeared to *redly.*" This awkward locution, as we have emphasized, has the theoretical advantage of suggesting that appearing is a process, that the adverb "redly" designates a property of a process (just as "swiftly" and "slowly" designate proper-

---

[13] Thomas Case, *Physical Realism* (London: Longmans, Green & Company, Ltd., 1888), pp. 24, 25, 33.

[14] Quoted by H. H. Price, *Perception* (New York: Robert M. McBride & Co., 1933), p. 127.

[15] *The Philosophy of Mind*, p. 163.

ties of processes), and that the process of being appeared to does not involve a *second* process which is the *experiencing* of the process of being appeared to.

What now does this second version of the "identity theory" tell us? What is involved in saying that that process which is Jones's being appeared to redly is really something that is to be found in his brain?

Let us consider how the theory might be applied to a single case—to just one occasion of Jones's being appeared to redly. The theory would tell us that on this occasion (1) there is going on in Jones's head a certain process—some kind of vibration, say—which a neurologist might be able to identify independently, and (2) that this neurological process is the very same process as the one that we are now describing as Jones's being appeared to redly. Case professed to give a "physical" account of the appearances that a man may experience but *not* of that process or event which is the man's experiencing of those appearances. The present view dispenses with the appearances and professes to give a physical account of experiencing—a physical account of that process or event which is Jones's being appeared to.[16]

I believe we can make five general points about the significance of this version of the identity theory. (1) It would be very difficult even to imagine circumstances under which any set of crucial experiments could be said to establish the theory beyond reasonable doubt—to show that Jones's being appeared to redly is identical with a vibration, say, in Jones's brain.[17] (2) Although no one knows whether the theory is true or false, the theory is nevertheless *confirmed* by such evidence as there is for saying that each specific instance of appearing is dependent upon a certain specific neurological process. (3) In saying that there is only one process where it might commonly be thought there are two, the theory does effect a reduction of entities. In other words, to the extent that the theory can be defended it can be said to "explain away" the need for supposing that there are two processes—that of being appeared to and *also* a certain neurological process—instead of only one. (4) But it does not "explain away" the process of being appeared to any more than it "explains away" the particular neurological process. If we knew

---

[16] The following procedure would yield a third version of the identity theory. Return to the sense-datum terminology; identify appearances, as Case did, with parts of physical objects inside the head (avoiding the errors attributed to Case); and then identify the experiencing of appearances (as the second version of the identity theory identifies being appeared to) with some process or event that is known to physiology. Our comments on the second version of the identity theory will also apply to this one.

[17] This fact has led some philosophers to suggest that the sentences formulating the identity theory are meaningless and that therefore the theory is neither true nor false. Cf. Norman Malcolm, "Scientific Materialism and the Identity Theory," *Dialogue*, III (1964), 115-25.

that the theory were true, then we would know something about certain neurological processes that no one knows now, namely, that they take place redly.[18] (5) Nor would the truth of the identity theory guarantee that what we know about appearances can be accommodated to the assumption that there is "nothing in the world but increasingly complex arrangements of physical constituents." In formulating the theory, we presuppose that there is such an entity as the *person* who is being appeared to; the process that the identity theory would identify with a neurological process is, in our particular example, that of Jones's being appeared to redly. What is directly evident to Jones, it will be recalled, is the fact that *he* is being appeared to redly. The identity theory does not itself imply that Jones is identical with any physical body or with any property, state, or process of any physical body.[19] And therefore, if we could show the identity theory to be true, we would not thereby be able to show that the facts of the matter, so far as appearing is concerned, involve only physical bodies and their properties, states, and processes.

[18] This point is clearly made by J. T. Stevenson in "Sensations and Brain Processes," *Philosophical Review*, LXIX (1960), 505-10.

[19] One might hope to show independently that sentences ostensibly about Jones can be translated into sentences which do not mention Jones but mention what we now call Jones's body. Such a "reductive" theory of the person involves difficulties like those involved in the various "reductive" theories discussed in Chap. 4. Cf. Sydney Shoemaker, *Self-Knowledge and Self-Identity* (Ithaca: Cornell University Press, 1963), and Roderick M. Chisholm, "Notes on the Awareness of the Self," *The Monist*, Vol. 49 (1965), 28-35.

WHAT IS TRUTH?

7

The answer   Our question is easy to answer if we allow ourselves a certain meta-physical assumption; otherwise, I believe, it is not. The assumption is that *states of affairs* may be said to exist, or not to exist, and that every belief and assertion (with certain exceptions to be noted) is a belief or assertion, with respect to some state of affairs, that that state of affairs exists.

A state of affairs may be identified obliquely as that to which propositional clauses refer. Thus, the propositional clauses in "Jones believes the road to be clear," "Smith denies what Jones believes, for Smith denies that the road is clear," and "The road's being clear is a necessary condition for a prompt arrival" refer to one and the same state of affairs. But they do not tell us whether or not that state of affairs exists, for they do not tell us whether or not the road is clear. States of affairs may consist of "unchanges" as well as changes; and as we have noted earlier, they may be compounded out of other states of affairs, just as propositional clauses may be compounded, by means of conjunction and disjunction, out of other propositional clauses.

Our answer, then, to the question "What is truth?" is this:

A *belief* or *assertion is true* provided, first, that it is a belief or assertion with respect to a certain state of affairs that that state of affairs exists, and provided, secondly, that that state of affairs does exist; and *a belief* or *assertion is false* provided, first, that it is a belief or assertion with respect to a certain state of affairs that that state of affairs exists, and provided, secondly, that that state of affairs does not exist. *It is true that* a given state of affairs exists provided that that state of affairs exists; and *it is false that* a given state of affairs exists provided that that state of affairs does not exist. And *a truth*, finally, is a state of affairs that exists.[1]

These definitions allow us to make three fundamental points concerning the nature of truth. (1) If it is *true* that Socrates is mortal, then it is a *fact* that Socrates is mortal. For a *fact*, in one sense of the term, may be said to be a state of affairs that exists (though in another sense of the term, it would be a state of affairs that is known to exist). Thus, we may say, as many philosophers have said, that "truths and facts are one and the same." (2) If it is *true* that Socrates is mortal, then Socrates *is* mortal. Thus, we may say, as many philosophers have said, that the sentential prefix "it is true that," is redundant (from which it does not follow, however, that "it is false that," "true," "false," "truth," or "falsity" is redundant). (3) If a man believes or asserts that Socrates is mortal, then, what he thus believes or asserts is true if, and only if, Socrates *is* mortal. Thus, the definitions enable us to preserve what is perhaps the only clear sense of the traditional "Veritas est adaequatio rei et intellectus": a true belief or assertion is one that "corresponds with the facts."

These three points, indeed, could be said to comprise conditions of adequacy for any account of truth. If we find an account of truth which is such that, according to that account, one or the other of these three points would be false, then we may say that that account is itself false.[2]

But our own account also has limitations.

States of affairs? Our answer to the question "What is truth?" refers not only to "states of affairs," but also to "states of affairs that exist" and "states of affairs that do not exist." We must say, for example, that among the entities that exist are Socrates' being mortal, there being horses, there being no unicorns; and we must say that among the entities that do not exist are Socrates' not being mortal, there being no horses, and there being unicorns. An account of truth that spoke only of con-

---

[1] Except for terminology, the theory of truth embodied by these definitions is essentially similar to the theories of such authors as: Bernard Bolzano, *Wissenschaftslehre* Vol. I (Leipzig: Felix Meiner, 1929), Secs. 19-33, first published in 1837; A. Meinong, *Über Annahmen*, 2nd ed. (Leipzig: Johann Ambrosius Barth, 1910), Chap. 3; C. A. Baylis, "Facts, Propositions, Exemplification and Truth," *Mind*, LVII (1948), 459-79. There may be reason (depending upon our theory of time) for replacing "exists" throughout, in the above definitions, by "exists, has existed, or will exist"; but for simplicity, we shall ignore this possibility.

[2] Cf. Alfred Tarski's account of the conditions of "material adequacy" that must be satisfied by any adequate theory of truth; "The Semantic Conception of Truth," *Philosophy and Phenomenological Research*, IV (1944), 341-75; reprinted in H. Feigl and W. S. Sellars, ed., *Readings in Philosophical Analysis* (New York: Appleton-Century-Crofts, 1949).

crete individual things, if it were otherwise adequate, would be preferable to the one that we have given.

Actually, our own definition is an imitation of Aristotle's, and what Aristotle says may seem not to entangle us in such entities as states of affairs that exist and states of affairs that do not exist. Referring to the truth of assertions, he said: "To say of what is that it is not, or of what is not that it is, is false, while to say of what is that it is, or of what is not that it is not, is true." [3] Aristotle does make use of propositional clauses—"that it is" and "that it is not"—and it could be argued, with some plausibility, that what these clauses refer to are states of affairs. But his account is simpler than the one proposed here. He can tell us that believing or asserting that there are horses is true if, and only if, there *are* horses, and believing or asserting that there are no unicorns is true if, and only if, there are no unicorns. We do not find him saying "The being of horses exists" and "The being of unicorns does not exist" (much less "The nonbeing of unicorns does exist" and "The nonbeing of horses does not exist"). But how are we to interpret his definition in application to more complex beliefs and assertions—to the belief or assertion, say, that if there had been no assistance from the guerillas, the revolt would not have succeeded? If Aristotle's definition is to apply to this type of belief or assertion, then he must say that here, too, one is believing or asserting, with respect to a certain entity, that that entity exists or that it does not exist. But what could that entity be? It would have to be a state of affairs, namely, that state of affairs which is assistance from the guerillas being a necessary condition for the success of the revolt. [4]

It may be, of course, that some ingenious philosopher can formulate an adequate definition of "true" which does not refer to such entities as "states of affairs." But I think it is accurate to say that no philosopher has done so up to now. In the absence of any acceptable alternative, therefore, we must resign ourselves to a definition that refers to states of affairs that exist and to states of affairs that do not exist. However, we may take comfort in the fact that such entities as these seem also to be involved in any adequate account of the concepts of explanation, meaning, purpose, belief, causation, value, and desire. [5]

[3] *Metaphysics*, 1011b.

[4] Thus, Aristotle himself spoke of "being in the sense of the true" and "nonbeing in the sense of the false," which terms seem to have been his way of referring respectively to states of affairs that exist and to states of affairs that do not exist. See *Metaphysics*, Book V, Chap. 7; Book VI, chaps. 1, 3; and Book IX, Chap. 10.

[5] Perhaps the most thoroughgoing attempt to construct an adequate philosophy without reference to such entities as states of affairs has been Franz Brentano's. See his *Psychologie vom empirischen Standpunkt*, 2nd ed., II (Leipzig: Felix Meiner, 1925), 158-72, and his *Wahrheit und Evidenz* (Leipzig: Felix Meiner, 1930). The

The words "true" and "false"   Let us now consider how such *words* as "true" and "false" are used. "It is true that," when prefixed to a sentence that is being used to make an assertion, adds nothing but emphasis to what is accomplished by uttering or writing the sentence itself; but the sentence itself, when thus used, tells us, with respect to a certain state of affairs, that that state of affairs exists. "It is false that," when prefixed to a sentence that is being used to make an assertion, is normally so prefixed in order to make that assertion which could also be made by writing or uttering the negation of the sentence. "It is true," taken as a complete sentence, is intended to express agreement—agreement, normally, with what is asserted by means of some other sentence. "That is false," similarly, is intended to express disagreement—to assert, with respect to some state of affairs that has been asserted to exist, that that state of affairs does not exist.

It is sometimes said that *sentences* are what the words "true" and "false" properly apply to, and in this book we have spoken from time to time of sentences that are true or false. But if we say that sentences are true or false, *simpliciter* and without qualifications, then we must say that some sentences are both true and false at one and the same time; and saying this readily leads to confusion. The sentence "It is raining" may be true when used to formulate an assertion in one place at one time, and false when used to formulate an assertion in another place or at another time. It would be preferable, therefore, not to say of a sentence that it is true (or that it is false) *simpliciter*; we should say of it, rather, that it has uses or interpretations such that, in those uses or interpretations, it may formulate a belief in, or an assertion of, what is true (or what is false). We might thus speak of a sentence as being true (or false) "under a certain interpretation," meaning that the assertion or belief that the sentence would formulate, if it were given that interpretation, would be a belief or assertion that is true (or that is false).

The words "belief" and "assertion," however, are equivocal, sometimes being used to refer to *what* it is that is believed or asserted, and sometimes being used to refer to the *believing* or *asserting* of it. What *is* this thing that we designate by the phrase "*what* it is that is believed or asserted"? We must be wary of this type of question. (Compare "In saying that the average American parent has 2.8 children we are saying of something that it has 2.8 children. What could this something pos-

---

contrary position was taken by A. Meinong, in *Über Annahmen*. The controversy was revived in Oxford by J. L. Austin and P. F. Strawson. See Austin's *Philosophical Papers* (New York: Oxford University Press, 1961) and Strawson's "Truth," *Proceedings of the Aristotelian Society*, XXIV (1950), and a review and criticism of the controversy by myself, in "J. L. Austin's *Philosophical Papers*," *Mind*, LXXIII (1964).

sibly be?") The safest way to deal with our question would probably be to say that *what* a man believes is true is simply to say that his belief —his *believing*—is true. And according to our definitions, to say that a man's believing, on any occasion, is true is to say that the state of affairs that he then believes to exist does exist. And analogously for "false" and for "asserting." [6]

The words "true" and "false," at least in twentieth-century America, are not generally used in application to believing and asserting. One tends to say of a man's believing or asserting, that it is "correct" or "mistaken," and not that it is "true" or "false." We may adhere to traditional philosophical usage, however, and speak of "true" and of "false" believings and assertings (keeping in mind that what we say can also be put in terms of "correct" and "mistaken").

"Truth" may also be applied to what does not involve any actual believing or asserting; for as we have noted, our definitions allow us to say that "truths and facts are one and the same." [7]

There is still another sense of "true," sometimes called an "improper" sense, in which the word may be said to apply to everything. One may say that, for every property, a "true" exemplification of that property is anything that *does* exemplify that property. A man is a true friend if, and only if, he *is* a friend—if, and only if, it is *true* that he is a friend. Everything is thus a true exemplification of whatever it does exemplify. This use of "true" is, of course, redundant; it serves to express emphasis and ordinarily on occasions when there might be cause for doubting what it is that is being asserted.

The Epimenides

Any theory of truth should attempt to deal with the various versions of the ancient paradox called the "Epimenides," or the "Liar." [8]

Consider: (1) the assertion of the man who asserts that his assertion is false; or (2) the belief of the man who had been hypnotized

---

[6] Philosophers sometimes use such terms as "proposition" and "statement" to designate the "object" of believing and asserting. Introduction of these terms into our present discussion might mislead us into supposing needlessly that *in addition to* things, properties, and states of affairs, there are still other types of entity as well. But if we speak in the way proposed above, we avoid the risk of making this supposition. (Sentences in our earlier chapters using the word "proposition" may readily be transformed into sentences referring to states of affairs without using "proposition".) Cf. Richard Cartwright, "Propositions," in R. J. Butler, ed. *Analytical Philosophy* (New York: Barnes & Noble, Inc., 1962).

[7] Bernard Bolzano thus spoke of facts as being "truths-in-themselves"; *Wissenschaftslehre*, Sec. 25. Cf. E. Husserl, *Logische Untersuchungen*, 2nd ed., I (Halle: Max Niemeyer, 1928), 184.

[8] So called because Epimenides of Crete is reported to have said that all Cretans were liars. St. Paul wrote to Titus: "One of themselves, a prophet of their own, said 'Cretans are always liars, evil beasts, lazy gluttons.' This testimony is true. . . ." *Titus*, I, 12-13.

that the belief induced in him by the hypnotist, whatever it may have been, is false—and suppose that *that* is the belief that the hypnotist induced; or (3) the belief or assertion, say, on the part of Plato, that Socrates' belief or assertion is false—where Socrates' belief or assertion happens to be that whatever it is that Plato is believing or asserting is false.[9] In each case, the assumption that the assertion or belief in question is true (or correct) implies that the assertion or belief in question is false (or mistaken), and the assumption that it is false implies that it is true. Hence, if we say that the belief or assertion is true, or that it is false, we seem to violate the law of contradiction. But if we say that it is neither true nor false we seem to violate the law of excluded middle. The problem lies in finding a way of avoiding these undesirable consequences.

We have said that every belief or assertion, "with certain exceptions to be noted," is a belief or assertion, with respect to some state of affairs, that that state of affairs exists. Let us now say of those exceptions—those beliefs and assertions which are *not* beliefs and assertions, with respect to any state of affairs, that that state of affairs exists—that they are "defective" or "have no content." Our treatment of the Epimenides will be based upon the assumption that the beliefs and assertions giving rise to the paradox are all defective.[10]

We may put the point more exactly: Let us say that a belief or assertion *A* is "dependent for its content" upon a belief or assertion *B* (which may or may not be the same as *A*), provided that *A* is a belief or assertion to the effect that *B* is (or that *B* is not) a belief or assertion that is true, or to the effect that *B* is (or that *B* is not) a belief or assertion that is false. Let us say further that if a belief or assertion *A* is thus "dependent for its content" upon a belief or assertion *B*, and if *B* in turn is dependent for *its* content upon *A*, then both *A* and *B* are "without content," or "defective." And now let us assume that if a belief or assertion is thus defective, then it is *not* a belief or assertion, with respect to any state of affairs, that that state of affairs exists. The beliefs and assertions giving rise to the paradox will be defective, according to our definition, and therefore, according to our assumption, they will not be beliefs or assertions, with respect to any state of affairs, that that state of affairs exists. In this way, we avoid the paradox.

[9] This version of the paradox was formulated by Albertus Magnus; cf. Ernest A. Moody, *Truth and Consequence in Mediaeval Logic* (Amsterdam: North-Holland Publishing Company, 1953), p. 103.

[10] Cf. A. Meinong's doctrine of *defekte Gegenstände*, in his *Über emotionale Präsentation* (Vienna: Alfred Hölder, 1917), p. 20, and the doctrine of *cassatio*, or nullification, attributed to the thirteenth-century author, William of Shyreswood; see William and Martha Kneale, *The Development of Logic* (New York: Oxford University Press, Inc., 1962), p. 228.

For we have said, it will be recalled, that a belief or assertion is *true*, provided, first, that it is a belief or assertion, with respect to a certain state of affairs, that that state of affairs exists, and provided, secondly, that that state of affairs does exist. And we have said that a belief or assertion is *false* provided, first, that it is a belief or assertion, with respect to a certain state of affairs, that that state of affairs exists, and provided, secondly, that that state of affairs does *not* exist. Hence, we may now say of the beliefs and assertions giving rise to the paradox, that they are neither true nor false, for they are not beliefs or assertions, with respect to any state of affairs, that that state of affairs exists.

Since we avoid saying that the troublesome beliefs and assertions are true, and also avoid saying that they are false, we do not violate the law of contradiction. Nor do we violate the law of excluded middle, for this law does not tell us that every belief or assertion is either true or false. It tells us, rather, that for every state of affairs, either that state of affairs exists or that state of affairs does not exist, and either it is true that that state of affairs exists or it is false that that state of affairs exists; and for every thing and every property, either the thing has that property or the thing does not have that property.

Our treatment will also apply to paradoxical *sentences*. We have said that a sentence is true, in a certain interpretation or use, if, in that interpretation or use, it formulates a belief or assertion that is true; and a sentence is false, in a certain interpretation or use, if, in that interpretation or use, it formulates a belief or assertion that is false. Since the sentences in which our paradoxes are expressed do not formulate beliefs or assertions that are true, or beliefs or assertions that are false, then they, too, are neither true nor false.[11]

But any solution to the paradox will be at some cost, and ours is no exception: We must say that if I have a belief A to the effect that your belief B is defective, and if your belief B is a belief to the effect that my belief A is defective, then neither belief is true or false; this also holds true for assertions. Hence, we cannot say that a belief or assertion A, to the effect that a belief or assertion B is defective, is *true* if, and only if, B *is* defective; we must specify further that A be non-defective.

---

[11] Most contemporary treatments of the paradox pertain only to those versions of it that apply to *sentences,* and consist either in asserting (as we have done) something from which it follows that the troublesome sentences are neither true nor false, or in recommending that we make our philosophical assertions only in languages which do not permit the formulation of such sentences. But they provide no treatment for those more basic versions of the paradox that pertain to believing and asserting.

Pragmatism   Some philosophers—"pragmatists" and "instrumentalists"—have said that truth consists in a kind of satisfaction, and falsity, in a kind of dissatisfaction. What could this mean?

Actually, "pragmatism" and "instrumentalism" are versions of a theory concerning the nature of *believing*. But if this theory about the nature of believing is true, then the truth of a belief *is* a kind of satisfaction, and the falsity of a belief, a kind of dissatisfaction. According to the theory, to *believe* is to be prepared for, or set for, something occurring. To be prepared for, or set for, something occurring, the theory continues, is to be in a state that will be "fulfilled" or "satisfied" if, and only if, that something occurs, and "disrupted" or "disequilibrated" if, and only if, it does not occur. But the belief that the something will occur is *true* if, and only if, that something does occur; and therefore, the belief will lead to satisfaction if, and only if, it is true, and to dissatisfaction if, and only if, it is false.

Thus, William James said, in effect, that if a man believes that there are tigers in India, then he is prepared, or set, for tigers being in India. And if the man is so prepared or set, James continued, then he is in a state which is such that, if he were to go to India, then he would be disrupted, disequilibrated, or surprised if, and only if, there were *no* tigers there, and he would be fulfilled or satisfied if, and only if, there *were* tigers there. Hence, on this theory of the nature of believing, the man's belief is true if, and only if (should he go to India), it is one that would produce fulfillment or satisfaction, and false if, and only if (should he go to India), it is one that would produce disruption, disequilibration, or surprise. Therefore, the theory allows us to say both that there is a sense in which truth consists in "satisfaction" and falsity in "dissatisfaction," and also, as James pointed out, that a true belief is one that "corresponds with the facts." [12] But the theory of believing from which this theory is derived would seem itself to be false.

The basic difficulty is not, as is often supposed, that the requisite concepts of satisfaction and dissatisfaction are unclear. Rather, we cannot say, of any particular belief, that that particular belief will lead to satisfaction if, and only if, it is true, or that it will lead to dissatisfaction if, and only if, it is false. The satisfactions or dissatisfactions to which the man's belief may lead (however sympathetically we interpret these terms "satisfaction" and "dissatisfaction") will be a function, in part, of his *other* beliefs. And these other beliefs may combine with a true belief to produce dissatisfaction, or with a false belief, to produce satis-

---

[12] James's clearest statements are in Lecture VI of *Pragmatism* (New York: David McKay Co., Inc., 1907) and in Chap. 2 ("The Tigers in India") of *The Meaning of Truth* (New York: David McKay, Inc., 1909). Cf. John Dewey, *Logic: The Theory of Inquiry* (New York: Holt, Rinehart & Winston, Inc., 1938).

faction. Thus, the belief that there are tigers in India, even if it is true, need not lead to satisfaction (the man may encounter tigers, but mistakenly think that they are lions or that he is not in India) and it may even lead to dissatisfaction (he goes to Syria, finds no tigers, and mistakenly believes that he is in India).

Other more refined versions of "pragmatism" and "instrumentalism" seem to be subject to similar difficulties. I would say, therefore, that there is no clear sense in which truth can be said to consist in "satisfaction," and falsity, in "dissatisfaction."

The true and the evident Our definition of "true belief" could be said to formulate the *conditions of truth* for a belief: It tells us that the belief that a certain state of affairs exists is true, just on condition that that state of affairs does exist. Hence, to give the truth conditions for any belief, it is sufficient merely to express or formulate that belief. *Conditions of truth*, therefore, must be distinguished from *criteria of evidence*.

Clearly, a belief may be a belief in what is true without being a belief in what is evident. May we also say, conversely, that a belief may be a belief in what is evident without being a belief in what is true?

In the case of what we have called the "directly evident," conditions of truth and criteria of evidence may be said to coincide. If it is evident to a man that he thinks he sees a horse, then he does think he sees a horse; and if he does think he sees a horse, then it is evident to him that he thinks he sees a horse. But in the case of other beliefs, conditions of truth and criteria of evidence do not seem to coincide. If there are criteria for saying, with respect to the belief that it rained yesterday or the belief that it will rain tomorrow, that the belief is a belief in what is now evident, or that it is one for which we now have adequate evidence, these criteria do not themselves include the fact (if it is a fact) that it did rain yesterday or that it will rain tomorrow. Hence, if we are not to be sceptics, and if we are not to restrict the evident to what is directly evident, we must face the possibility that a belief may be a belief in what is evident, or a belief for which we have adequate evidence, and at the same time, be a belief in what is false.

But what is the good of evidence if that which is evident may also be false? [13] Is there anything we can do to secure a connection between the true and the evident? Here we have the kind of question that leads philosophers to construct "theories of reality." Consider the following three steps that we might take.

(1) We could begin by replacing our definition of "true belief"

[13] "If you place the nature of truth in one sort of character and its test in something quite different, you are pretty certain, sooner or later, to find the two falling apart." Brand Blanshard, *The Nature of Thought*, II (London: George Allen & Unwin, 1939), 268.

with one that defines the true in terms of the evident. For example, we could say, if a man believes, with respect to a certain state of affairs, that that state of affairs exists, then, what he thus believes is *true*, provided that what he thus believes would be *evident* to a being such that, for every state of affairs, either it is evident to that being that that state of affairs exists, or it is evident to him that that state of affairs does not exist.[14]

But this new definition of "true belief" lacks something that our earlier definition provided. It enabled us to say that if a man believes truly that Socrates is mortal, then Socrates *is* mortal. Therefore, we were able to say that a true belief is one that "corresponds with the facts." But our new definition provides no guarantee that if a man believes truly that Socrates is mortal, then Socrates *is* mortal. Hence, if we define truth in this way, we can no longer be sure that our true beliefs "correspond with the facts."

(2) To obtain the needed assurance, we may be tempted to take a second step—a step into metaphysics. For we could now add a theory about the nature of "the facts" by saying that Socrates *is* mortal provided that, for a being of the sort envisaged in the new definition of "true belief," the belief that Socrates is mortal is one that would be *evident*. That is to say, Socrates *is* mortal provided that these conditions hold: Any being such that, for every state of affairs, either it is evident to him that that state of affairs exists, or it is evident to him that that state of affairs does not exist, would be a being for whom it would be evident that Socrates is mortal. In this case, we could say not only that if it is evident to such a being that Socrates is mortal then Socrates is mortal, but also, that if it is true that Socrates is mortal, then Socrates is mortal. And thus, we would arrive at a theory of reality—a theory that has taken various forms in the history of philosophy—that could be summarized by saying: The being who judges with evidence is "the measure of all things." [15]

[14] "Truth pertains to the judgment of the person . . . who judges about a thing in the way in which anyone whose judgments were *evident* would judge about the thing; hence it pertains to the judgment of one who asserts what the person whose judgments are *evident* would also assert." Franz Brentano, *Wahrheit und Evidenz*, p. 139.

[15] Considerations such as these led Charles Sanders Peirce to conclude that "the reality of that which is real does depend on the real fact that investigation is destined to lead, at last, if continued long enough, to a belief in it"; *Collected Papers*, Vol. V (Cambridge: Harvard University Press, 1934), 5.408 (cf. 5.358n., 5.494, 5.565). Franz Brentano's theory (see his *Wahrheit und Evidenz*) may be interpreted in a similar way, and perhaps, too, the doctrine of the stoics, who held that a "real object is one that is capable of giving rise to an apprehensive presentation"; quoted by Sextus Empiricus, *Outlines of Pyrrhonism*, Book III, in Vol. I of *Sextus Empiricus*, The Loeb Classical Library (Cambridge: Harvard University Press, 1933), p. 487.

But how are we to assure ourselves that a belief that is evident to *us* is one that would also be evident to a being for whom all truths are evident? Our metaphysician would have us take one more step.

(3) We will now be asked to assume not only that there is such a being, a being for whom all truths are evident, but also, that each of us is identical with that being, and therefore, with each other. This, in its essentials, is what I take to be the theory of reality underlying what has been called the "coherence theory of truth." [16]

Such a theory is a very high price to pay for the desired connection between the true and the evident (though it is also thought to contribute toward the solution of certain metaphysical problems). It conflicts, moreover, with Aristotle's basic insight: "It is not because we think truly that you are pale, that you *are* pale; it is because you *are* pale that we who say this have the truth." [17] I cannot feel, therefore, that it is reasonable for anyone to accept the theory. But if we reject the theory, we must find some other way of dealing with the problems it was designed to solve.

[16] Among the clearest statements of the theory are: H. H. Joachim, *The Nature of Truth* (New York: Oxford University Press, Inc., 1906) and *Logical Studies* (New York: Oxford University Press, Inc., 1948), especially Chap. 3; Brand Blanshard, *The Nature of Thought*. The three steps I have set forth oversimplify the theory considerably; the identity asserted in the final step, for example, is usually qualified in some way or other, making the thesis somewhat difficult to grasp. The "coherence theory," moreover, is also a theory of evidence, implying that something similar to what Carneades called "concurrence" constitutes the sole criterion of evidence; but according to Carneades, and according to what we have said in Chap. 3, concurrence does not constitute the sole criterion of evidence.

[17] *Metaphysics*, 1051b.

INDEX

A

Acceptability, 18, 22, 41-43
"Adverbial theory," the, 95-102
Agnosticism, 22n; *see also* Scepticism
Albertus Magnus, 108n
Analogy, 64
Analytic statements, 84-90
"Animal faith," 48
Anscombe, G. E. M., 29n
A posteriori knowledge, 73-75
Appearances, 30-37, 43n, 47, 91-102
A priori knowledge, 73-78, 83-84
Aristotle, 7, 25, 32, 46, 75-76, 94, 105, 113
Augustine, St., 21, 30-31, 43n
Austin, J. L., 15-18, 31, 92n, 106n
Ayer, A. J., 13

B

"Basic propositions," 23n
Baylis, C. A., 104n
Behaviorism, 65n
Blanshard, Brand, 111n, 113n
Bolzano, Bernard, 9n, 104n, 107n
Bradley, F. H., 100
Brentano, Franz, 28n, 51n, 89n, 105-6n, 112n
Broad, C. D., 97

C

Carnap, Rudolf, 9n, 82n
Carneades, 41-45, 52-54, 113n

Cartwright, Richard, 107n

Cartwright, Richard, 107n
Case, Thomas, 99-101
Certainty, 23n
Church, Alonzo, 79n
Cicero, 44n
Clifford, W. K., 18-19
Coffey, P., 13n
"Coherence theory," 113
"Common sensibles," 32, 46-47
"Commonsensism," 57
Concurrence, 42-44, 49, 53-54, 113n
Confirmation, 52-53
Criteria of knowing, 56-69
"Critical cognitivism," 61-62, 66, 68

D

Defeasibility, 48
Defective beliefs, 108-9
Democritus, 91-94
Demonstrative knowledge, 78
Descartes, René, 12n, 25n, 30-31, 58, 78n
Dewey, John, 110
Dilthey, Wilhelm, 65n
Ducasse, C. J., 28n, 95n

E

Empiricism, 45, 52, 56
Epistemic logic, 22n
Epistemic terms, 18-22